RUSSIA AND CENTRAL ASIA

The Central Asian and Caucasian Prospects project is sponsored by:

- A. Meredith Jones & Co. Ltd.
- BG plc
- British Aerospace plc
- British American Tobacco
- The British Petroleum Company plc
- ENI S.p.A.
- Mobil Oil Company Ltd.
- Shell International Petroleum Company Limited
- Statoil

Series editor: Edmund Herzig
Head, Russia and Eurasia Programme: Roy Allison

RUSSIA AND CENTRAL ASIA
A New Web of Relations

Lena Jonson

THE ROYAL INSTITUTE OF
INTERNATIONAL AFFAIRS
Russia and Eurasia Programme

ISBN 1 86203 022 7

Typeset in Times by Koinonia, Manchester
Printed and bound in Great Britain by the Chameleon Press Limited
Cover design by Youngs Design in Production

CONTENTS

Tables

ABOUT THE AUTHOR

Lena Jonson is a Senior Research Fellow at the Swedish Institute of International Affairs in Stockholm. She wrote this study as a researcher in the Russia and Eurasia Programme at the Royal Institute of International Affairs. She has written extensively on Russian foreign and security policy. Her latest publications include *The Tajik War: A Challenge to Russian Policy* (RIIA, 1998), *Peacekeeping and the Role of Russia in Eurasia* (co-edited volume, 1996), and 'In Search of a Doctrine: Russian Interventionism in Conflicts in Its "Near Abroad"' (*Low-Intensity Conflict and Law Enforcement*, winter 1996).

ACKNOWLEDGMENTS

I would like to thank Roy Allison for suggesting and encouraging me to write this paper as well as Edmund Herzig for his professional and editorial assistance, and Bridget Martyn and Margaret May for improving the English of the final text.

I am grateful for the valuable advice offered by members of the study group convened for the first draft of the paper and especially for the contributions and information from Rosemarie Forsythe, Keun-Wook Paik and Michael Kaser. My research for this paper was also greatly assisted by the opportunities offered during 1997–8 in the context of my work as a Senior Research Fellow for the Chatham House project 'Keeping the Peace in the CIS', supported by the Ford Foundation.

October 1998   L.J.

SUMMARY

Seven years after the break-up of the Soviet Union the political scene in Central Asia is changing. The new states are expanding their relations with the outside world. At the same time, Russia is facing an *involuntary disengagement* from the region. In this process Russia is rapidly and involuntarily losing influence because of factors beyond its control. The process is reflected in the commercial, the military-security and the cultural fields as well as with regard to natural resources (exploitation of oil and gas) and transport systems.

Whether Russia, as an outcome of this process, becomes marginalized in Central Asian politics depends on its capacity to adapt and formulate a policy more appropriate to the new situation.

This study analyses Russia's search for a policy towards the Central Asian states of Kazakhstan, Uzbekistan, Turkmenistan, Kyrgyzstan and Tajikistan. It discusses the prospects for Russian policy in Central Asia in all of the above-mentioned fields.

A conclusion of the study is that Russian policy in Central Asia during 1996 became more pragmatic and 'low-profile' because of an awareness of Russia's weakened position in the region. At the same time it shifted from a *political* strategy to an *economic* strategy. Russia maintained, however, a *zero-sum* perspective on the growing influence of out-of-region actors in Central Asia. This was evident as energy issues in 1997 came to the fore and Russia tried to counter its waning influence. A crucial question for the future is whether Russia will abandon this perspective in favour of a *cooperative* one, thereby participating as a partner in the ongoing realignment of Central Asia. The role of commercial interests in general and of certain companies in particular may be decisive as they act as lobby groups influencing government policy.

The economic crisis which erupted in August 1998 may speed up the process of involuntary disengagement by Russia but slow down, perhaps only temporarily, its shift towards a cooperative perspective and a new policy in an effort to adapt to the changing situation in Central Asia.

Regional Map

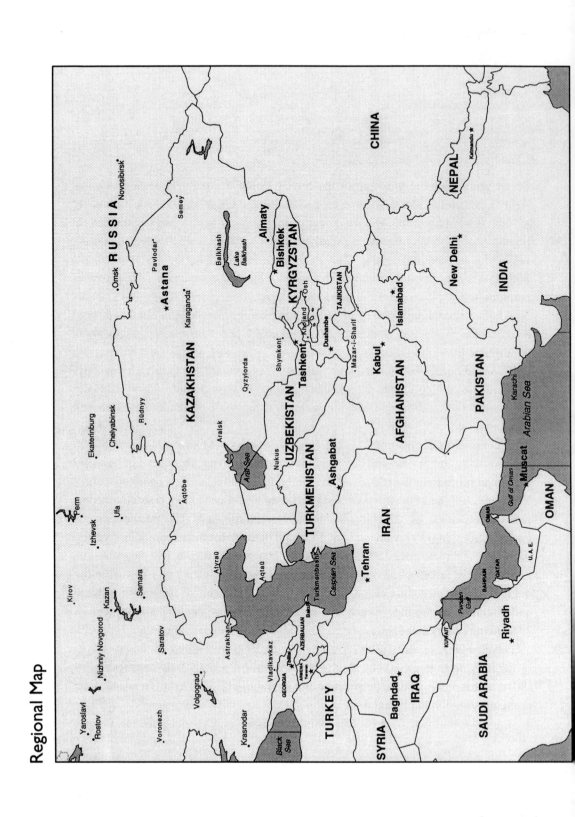

1 INTRODUCTION: TOWARDS INVOLUNTARY DISENGAGEMENT?

Seven years after the break-up of the Soviet Union the political scene in Central Asia is rapidly changing. There is a continuing process of what here will be called an involuntary Russian disengagement from Central Asia. It is a process of disengagement in the sense that Russia is rapidly losing its influence on the region. It is involuntary because it is caused by factors beyond Russian control. Russia has been the dominant power in Central Asia for more than a century and still is the strongest foreign power in the region. Its influence is now waning relative to that of other countries. This may be considered a natural process following the break-up of the Soviet empire. For Russia it is a painful experience. Just how radical a break with the past it will be and how marginalized Russia will become in Central Asian politics are as yet unknown. Both are contingent on Russia's capability to adapt to the new situation and formulate a policy that is more appropriate.

At the time of writing, Russia is still searching for a policy towards the new states of the former Soviet Union. The task of this paper is to discuss the prospects for Russian policy in Central Asia and, more specifically, to analyse Russia's search for a policy towards the Central Asian states of Kazakhstan, Uzbekistan, Turkmenistan, Kyrgyzstan and Tajikistan.

The trend towards Russian disengagement is contingent on the natural resources and transportation systems of the former Soviet territory. It is reflected in the commercial, military, security and cultural fields, and can briefly be characterized as follows:

- *The commercial field.* Russia has not been successful in creating economic integration within the Commonwealth of Independent States (CIS) in general or with the Central Asian states in particular. The relative importance of trade between Russia and the Central Asian states is decreasing as other trading partners become more important to the latter. Hardly any Russian private capital other than in the energy sector is being invested in Central Asia. There are signs of a new economic network appearing at local level in Asian relations.
- *The military-security field.* Russia has not been able to integrate the Central Asian states militarily, and its proposals for the military integration of the CIS

1

are being rejected. Without national armies after the break-up of the Soviet Union, the Central Asian states had signed bilateral agreements with Russia on military cooperation and border defence. However, there is now a trend towards a diminished Russian military presence. Turkmenistan and Uzbekistan are the countries most determined to reduce their military dependence on Russia. Kazakhstan has developed close military cooperation with Russia, but is also looking in other directions for security guarantees. All the Central Asian states except Tajikistan are members of the NATO Partnership for Peace Programme.

- *The cultural field.* The Russian population in these countries will always guarantee a degree of Russian cultural presence. However, as the former decreases and Central Asian governments promote their own cultural heritage, Russian cultural influence must in time diminish.

- *The field of natural resources and transport systems.* Russia's role in the exploitation of gas and oil is being reduced to the rank of only one among several players. Russia still maintains control over the pipeline systems. However, as international consortia gain the rights to exploitation of oil and gas, agreements are being signed for new pipeline systems to be built along routes that do not cross Russia – to the east and to the south. Railways and roads are being extended and linked to neighbouring countries, thereby helping them to diversify their contacts with the outside world.

Several factors explain this trend of an involuntary disengagement by Russia. First, the break-up of the Soviet Union created independent states pursuing interests which they perceive as different from those of Russia. A determination exists among Central Asian leaders to reduce dependence on Russia and to avoid any commitment to deeper integrative structures with their powerful neighbour. Second, Central Asian leaders are seeking integration within wider international cooperative structures. The effort to establish the engagement of non-CIS powers in the region can also be seen as part of the Central Asian leadership's conscious balancing of interests and influence in the region. Third, Russia has been unable to sustain its influence following the break-up of the Soviet Union, owing, in part, to a lack of economic and military resources. However, a potent factor here is Russia's own lack of an appropriate policy towards Central Asia. Fourth, there is considerable interest in the Central Asian region from further afield, with various governments and companies offering support and encouragement. There are thus now potential global investors and partners – from Russia to the north, Europe and the USA to the west, the Middle East and South Asia to the south and China, Korea and Japan to the east. Where Russia once had a free hand in Central Asia, it now has to compete under radically different circumstances.

2

Fifth, the prospects for exploitation of the wealth of Central Asian gas and oil resources have initiated a 'new great game' to gain influence, control and profits. Immediately after the break-up of the Soviet Union discussions were initiated with foreign companies on the exploitation of Central Asian oil and gas resources and the new feasibility of transport routes to markets in Europe and Asia. During 1997 these discussions entered a more concrete phase as memoranda and agreements were signed opening up prospects for pipelines in different geographical directions. The first deliveries along new routes soon followed.

Central Asia's energy resources constitute only a minor part of the total energy resources of the world. However, against the background of growing global demand they have gained greater importance. To Russia, they constitute both a possibility for Russian investments and a threat of new competition for the same markets. They form the basis for growing foreign interest in the region and provide the Central Asian states with the potential for an independent foreign policy and a new reorientation. As a result, cooperation has developed not only on a regional level but also among the Central Asian states and other CIS states without the participation of Russia.

Russia has not been able to formulate a policy that is attractive to the Central Asian states. It has shown confusion over what constitutes Russian interests in Central Asia and in the implementation of those interests. What is more, Russia has less to offer in a situation where the Central Asians are free to develop relations of partnership and assistance elsewhere.

Traditionally, Russian understanding of the world is powerfully influenced by an element of geostrategic thinking which it retains to this day. In the discussion of Russian policy change two sets of paired concepts will be used. The concepts of *'zero-sum perspective'* and *'cooperative perspective'* will be used with regard to Russia's approach to the role and influence of non-CIS states in Central Asia. The concepts of *'political strategy'* and *'economic strategy'* describe the principal means used by Russia to strengthen its position in Central Asia.

According to the 'zero-sum perspective', competition between states and state interests is seen as a zero-sum game in which the gains of one side are the losses of the other. The essence of international politics is thus reduced to a struggle between the main centres of power for control over territories, although the attempts at control may vary and both military and political forms may be used.[1] From such a perspective Russia observes with concern all processes in Central Asia where non-CIS states gain influence, and regards them as a victory for an anti-Russian front set

---

[1] See A. Torkunov, who uses the categories 'geopolitics' and 'geo-economics' in the discussion arranged by the journal *International Affairs* at the beginning of 1996. 'National Interests in Russian Foreign Policy', *International Affairs* (Moscow), vol. 42, no. 2, 1996.

up by foreign powers with the objective of undermining Russia.[2] A 'cooperative' perspective differs in that it appreciates the opportunities opening up for Russia as a result of the larger international interest in Central Asia. From a 'cooperative' perspective an increased international interest in Central Asia does not in itself constitute a threat to Russian interests.

The term 'political strategy' will be used to characterize a policy according to which priority is given to political and military means and levers. An 'economic strategy' gives priority to economic strength and economic levers as the best instruments for power and influence in foreign regions. In an attempt to describe the requirements for a state to compete successfully for influence under the new international conditions after the end of the Cold War, a Russian scholar writes,

> the period of large political-ideological projects with a military cushion, typical of the Cold War, is gone. In today's world with all its political and socio-cultural heterogeneity, considerations of market economy efficiency become the absolute determinant for the conduct not only of private business but also of states. The strength (or weakness) of a state is determined by how successfully it manages to enter the accelerating process of an economization of international relations and correspondingly to subordinate its activity to the demands of the global economy.[3]

In contrast to the 'zero-sum perspective', strategies within a 'cooperative' perspective imply a normal state-to-state policy of developing mutually beneficial contacts and pursuing commercial and national interests rather than emphasizing strategic considerations arising from the interplay of great and regional powers in the region.

To understand the dynamics of Russian foreign policy-making it is important to take into account the new influences on it. To the traditional cast, new actors have been added. Besides the president, the government, the military and other state structures, powerful economic and financial groups have assumed an important role, even though they are not officials of the Russian government. First and foremost they include the huge Russian gas monopoly Gazprom and the large oil companies. Policy takes shape in the dynamic interplay of overlapping and diverging interests between these groups and the Russian government. Moreover, a study of Russian relations and policy with regard to Central Asia would not be complete if the local

---

[2] A good example of this perspective is the 1994 report by the SVR (the Russian Foreign Intelligence Service) and its former director, 'Nuzhdaetsya li v korrektirovke pozitsiya Zapada?', *Rossiiskaya gazeta*, 24 September 1994.

[3] O. Reznikova, 'Rossiya, Turtsiya i Iran v Tsentralnoi Azii', *Mirovaya ekonomika i mezhdunarodnye otnosheniya*, 1997, no. 1.

4

level of contacts between Russian and Central Asian provinces were not also taken into account. Russian regions have a great deal of independence from the centre to initiate moves in developing their own relations with neighbouring countries.

Chapter 2 assesses the challenge to Russian policy posed by the new network of international relations in Central Asia, while Chapter 3 depicts the main directions in Russia's search for a policy towards the region. In the following chapters Russian policies with regard to military and security issues, cultural issues, economic cooperation, and energy issues are analysed. The last chapter summarizes the changes in Russia's search for a policy towards Central Asia, and discusses the prospects for future Russian influence in Central Asia. This study concludes that Russian policy in Central Asia has shifted from a political to an economic strategy within a continuing zero-sum perspective on the world. The 'new great game' of energy in Central Asia has contributed greatly to such a shift. The crucial question for the future is whether Russia will be able to abandon its zero-sum perspective in favour of a cooperative one with regard to the continuing changes in Central Asia.

2 THE CHALLENGE: A REALIGNMENT OF RELATIONS

Characteristics of the Central Asian states

The break-up of the Soviet Union was not welcomed by the Central Asian republics. All except Kazakhstan declared independence in the months after the August 1991 coup in Moscow, but, with the possible exception of Uzbekistan, they viewed their independence as a means of maximizing their room for manoeuvre *vis-à-vis* the central authorities in Moscow rather than as a statement of intent to 'go it alone'.[1] Broadly speaking, Central Asia could at that time be described as more conservative than other parts of the Soviet Union. In the elections of 1989 and 1990 the Soviet pattern of presenting only one candidate for each constituency was still largely maintained in Central Asia. A mobilized national identity had developed only within a small group of the political leadership and of the intelligentsia, but was not widespread.

Of paramount importance to the Central Asian leaders was the maintenance of economic assistance from Russia, which in turn favoured close links with Russia within a new Commonwealth. Prior to the break-up of the Soviet Union they had begun a tentative search for contacts with the outside world for investment to supplement or replace the slowly declining economic support from Moscow. They nourished the hope that independence would bring foreign capital and investments to the region from governments and companies interested in new markets and business opportunities. The idea of a 'diversification' of relations with the outside world thus already existed in embryo. Turkey and Iran were looked upon as the two states which for reasons of cultural affinity and geographical closeness would play a large role in the future of Central Asia. They were perceived as representing two politically different models, with Turkey as the secular and Iran as the theocratic state. However, neither was economically strong enough to make an impact on the Central Asian political map, and neither turned out to be culturally attractive. During 1993–4 a trend towards reintegration with Russia became noticeable. Russia had become more forceful, and the Central Asians turned to it once again,

---

[1] Bess A. Brown, 'Security Concerns of the Central Asian States', in Jed C. Snyder, ed., *After Empire: The Emerging Geopolitics of Central Asia*, Washington, DC, National Defense University Press, 1995, p. 68.

disillusioned with their expectations of economic assistance from the outside world.

1995 marks a dividing line in Central Asian relations with the outside world; a more pronounced policy of 'diversification' became evident in 1996 and 1997. A main factor behind this change was a growing awareness among Central Asian leaders that Russia would not be able to deliver what the region needed in the way of economic assistance, which would have to be found elsewhere instead.

Today the general trend among the Central Asian states is still to try to 'diversify' relations with the outside world. However, Central Asia is not a homogeneous region and it is essential to take account of the differences between the various states to understand their policies towards Russia. Kazakhstan is the only one which shares a border with Russia – more than 6,000 km long, as opposed to the 1,700 km border with China. Kazakhstan's Russian population constitutes as much as 36 per cent of the total and is spread over all of the country's nineteen regions, although its concentration is highest in the cities and the northern and northeastern parts of the country.[2] These factors account in part for the high priority given to relations with Russia in the policy of any Kazakhstani government.

Uzbekistan has no borders with Russia and is landlocked. Its territory is not as large as Kazakhstan's but it has the largest population in Central Asia and the potential to become a great power regionally. Russia has always been wary of Uzbekistan's potential position of influence. The Russian population constituted only six per cent of the total in 1994.[3] Turkmenistan's territory is large, second only to that of Kazakhstan, but it has a small population of which ethnic Russians constitute eight per cent. It has long borders with Iran and Afghanistan and access to the Caspian Sea. Kyrgyzstan and Tajikistan are both landlocked, and cut off from Russia through vast territories of other Central Asian states. They are both small and have small populations. Kyrgyzstan's Russian population represents as much as 17 per cent of the total, in contrast to Tajikistan, from which most Russians have fled. Both countries' sensitive geographical location between Uzbekistan and China, and their closeness to the conflict in Afghanistan, have made them look to Russia for security and assistance. The regime in Tajikistan with its endemic civil war between 1992 and 1997 became completely dependent on Russian assistance. All the Central Asian states have large national minorities – another factor for potential instability in these countries.

---

[2] In 1991 Russians made up more than 50 per cent of the population in nine of the northern oblasts. In the capital, Almaty, they still account for some 80 per cent of the population.
[3] Olivier Roy, *La nouvelle Asie Centrale ou la fabrication des nations*, Editions du Seuil, Paris, 1997, p. 27.

'Diversification' – foreign policy shifts in Central Asia

The general trend in Central Asian politics towards diversifying foreign relations is reflected both in more outspoken statements by the Central Asian leaders criticizing Russian policy and in the way these countries try to develop external contacts. The trend is well illustrated by the case of Kazakhstan's relations with Russia and in statements by President Nazarbayev, who for a long time remained Russia's most loyal partner and a solid supporter of CIS integration.

Despite the central importance to his country of relations with Russia, Nazarbayev, in an interview in the Russian newspaper *Nezavisimaya gazeta* in January 1997, expressed bitterness towards Russian policies and clearly showed his disappointment with the CIS: 'So far we hear from Russia different kinds of unfounded demands but we do not feel a real effort to cooperate with mutual benefit ... On some issues within the CIS Russia is pursuing a destructive policy, and is distancing potential allies rather than attracting them'. His concluding words were a warning to Russia that 'today it is necessary to radically reform not only the CIS but also Russian policy towards its closest neighbours. As long as this policy is not truly responsible and friendly ... CIS states will continue to be attracted by and orient themselves towards other geopolitical centres.'[4]

As early as 1991[5] Nazarbayev had introduced the concept of a multivector foreign policy to describe the need for diversification of relations with the outside world and cooperation with partners in all geographical directions. However, not until 1994 did the concept receive a more pronounced place in Kazakhstan's foreign policy. As Nazarbayev became more determined in his efforts to seek partners in economic development wherever he could find them, the interests of the two countries started to diverge. A rift in relations with Russia developed.

Commentators in the Russian media criticized this new shift in foreign policy, claiming early in 1996 that Kazakhstan 'had distanced itself from Russia to such an extent that on several issues there is no point in having any dealings with it'.[6] The Russian media started to attack Nazarbayev for moving closer to Ukraine, Georgia, Azerbaijan and Uzbekistan, all states determined to reduce their dependence on Russia.[7]

[4] 'Nursultan Nazarbayev, "Rossiya mogla by stat sterzhnem sodruzhestva, no ne stala",' *Nezavisimaya gazeta*, 16 January 1997, pp. 1, 3. In an interview in November 1996 Nazarbayev denied any change in Kazakh foreign policy. On the question of whether Kazakhstan had turned its back on Russia, he diplomatically stressed Kazakhstan's foreign policy of developing relations in all directions. 'Ya s bolshim optimizmom smotryu na budushchee otnoshenii Kazakhstana i Rossii', *Nezavisimaya gazeta*, 11 November 1996, pp. 1, 3.

[5] Nursultan Nazarbayev, *Bez pravykh i levykh*, Moscow, Molodaya gvardiya, 1991.

[6] Radzhab Safarov, 'Rossiya ukhodit ottuda, otkuda ee ne gnali', *Nezavisimaya gazeta*, 6 January 1996, p. 3.

[7] The Russian nationalist paper *Zavtra* in September 1996 severely criticized Nazarbayev for changing most aspects of Kazakh foreign policy. Other papers followed. See *Zavtra*, September 1997; and *Inside Central Asia*, no. 146, 4–10 November 1996, p. 5.

In May 1997 Aman Tuleyev, the Russian minister for relations with the CIS, characterized Nazarbayev as 'an energetic initiator of and participant in many blocs, projects and actions clearly of an anti-Russian orientation'.[8] When Chernomyrdin went to Almaty in October 1997 to restore relations, the Russian media described the meeting with Nazarbayev as 'maybe the most complicated negotiations during the last few years to try to find solutions to the numerous intense problems piling up between Kazakhstan and Russia'.[9] No solutions emerged from the meeting, but an intergovernmental commission was set up to focus on unresolved issues in bilateral relations. Nazarbayev stated in sharper phrasing than usual that 'both Kazakhstan and Russia have to get used to the fact that we now are different states and there will be no concessions against the interests of the people'.[10]

Uzbekistan, earlier than any of the other Central Asian states, showed a determination to reduce its dependence on Moscow and to reorient its foreign policy. Like the other Central Asian states, it kept a low profile in foreign policy statements during the first half of the 1990s; but even before the break-up of the Soviet Union it began a determined effort to achieve self-sufficiency with regard to energy supply and to increase its production of oil. By laying 1,000 kilometres of pipeline a year, drastically cutting domestic consumption and successfully seeking Western investment, Uzbekistan achieved this energy self-sufficiency in the second half of 1995, no longer having to rely on imports from Russia.

In June 1996 the Uzbek President Islam Karimov paid his first visit to the USA, thereby creating a watershed in his country's foreign policy. He managed to secure major deals with American companies for the development of Uzbekistan's natural resources. What was even more important was the strong support he received from the US leadership and US Defense Secretary William Perry, who described Uzbekistan as an 'important strategic partner of the US'. Uzbekistan, which in 1992 had been instrumental in helping Russia's extended arm to shift the balance of forces in the Tajik civil war, was now regarded by Moscow as a centre of an anti-Russian tendency in Central Asia. President Karimov started to distance himself more openly from the CIS by criticizing Russia's 'imperial plans' and rejecting proposals for CIS multilateral cooperation. Bilateral relations also declined. In September 1997, at the time of the visit of the Russian State Duma chairman Gennadii Seleznev, relations between the two countries were described as 'unsatisfactory'.[11]

During the first years of independence Turkmenistan mainly fell in line with Moscow. However, it had early demonstrated a preference for bilateral relations

---

[8] RIA (Russian News Agency), 20 May 1997; *Inside Central Asia*, no. 173, 19–25 May 1997, pp. 1 and 3.
[9] Sergei Kozlov, 'Nazarbayev bolshe ne nameren ustupat', *Nezavisimaya gazeta*, 7 October 1997, p. 3.
[10] Ibid.
[11] Radio Free Europe/Radio Liberty (RFE/RL) Newsline, no. 126, 26 September 1997.

with Russia instead of multilateral CIS cooperation. In 1993 it declared itself a 'neutral' country and in December 1995 the UN General Assembly recognized Turkmenistan's status of 'permanent neutrality'. As a consequence Turkmenistan distanced itself from most multilateral cooperative efforts. President Niyazov saw the potential in exploiting the huge resources of gas and oil in his country. Firmly determined to develop its economic potential, Turkmenistan adopted a policy to attract foreign investors for exploitation and to find routes for export to external markets. As Russia and Turkmenistan became potential rivals in the same markets for gas, their interests diverged. The conflict of interest over issues of energy resources, exploitation, export to external markets, and territorial disputes over the legal division of the Caspian Sea became central to Russian–Turkmen relations. The manner in which Moscow handled these issues during 1997 contributed to the further distancing of the two countries.

As already mentioned, both Kyrgyzstan and Tajikistan are heavily dependent on Russia; as small states in an insecure environment they look to it for military assistance. They have maintained a low profile in foreign policy statements and no serious crisis has developed in their bilateral relations with Russia. Kyrgyzstan was described in the Russian media in 1997 as 'loyal to Moscow but with a "wait-and-see attitude", with regard to integration in the CIS.[12] However, as will be shown below, the new network of international relations that is now developing is causing even Kyrgyzstan and Tajikistan to slowly orient themselves away from Russia and in new geographical directions.

The new regional network

After the break-up of the Soviet Union the Central Asians initiated a new mechanism of regional cooperation.[13] In July 1994 the Central Asian Union (CAU) was created by Kazakhstan, Uzbekistan and Kyrgyzstan. Tajikistan joined in April 1998 but Turkmenistan still remains outside the organization. Russia became an 'observer' in August 1996. The objective of the CAU is to create a common political, economic and cultural space through regional integration. An agreement on a Central Asian Economic Union (CAEU) was signed and a Central Asian Bank for Cooperation and Development was set up.[14] The four Central Asian countries share the same problems over trade barriers and separate economic regulations as

---

[12] Mekhman Gafarli, 'Tsentralno-aziatskii soyuz prevrashchaetsya v voennyi blok', *Nezavisimaya gazeta,* 20 December 1997, p. 3.
[13] Oumirserik Kasenov, 'Problems of Cooperation and Integration in Central Asia', *Central Asia Monitor,* 1997, no. 3.
[14] Several institutions have been created such as an Inter-State Council, a Council of Prime Ministers, Foreign Ministers and Defence Ministers, and an Executive Committee for the Inter-State Council.

the rest of the CIS. In contrast to the CIS, the members of the Central Asian Union seem more determined to overcome these problems and develop cooperation.[15] The member states have worked out cooperation with regard to several issues including the effective use of fuel, power and water resources, and the development of gas deposits, transport and communications.[16] In December 1997 Uzbekistan, Kazakhstan and Kyrgyzstan signed an agreement to establish a 'common economic space'.

The CAU can be seen both as a sub-grouping within the CIS, and as an alternative to it. The leaders of these states declare that the CAU is only the former, but it is obvious that they also view it as an alternative to the stagnating CIS. Kyrgyzstan's President Askar Akaev stated in December 1997 that 'the three countries, unlike the CIS, only undertake projects that can be carried out in practice'.[17]

As early as 1994 the Central Asian states started to hold meetings on military and security issues. An Inter-State Council consisting of Kazakhstan, Kyrgyzstan and Uzbekistan decided in December 1995 to establish a joint Council of Defence Ministers to consider issues of regional security and defence coordination, including the coordination of military exercises, air defence and defence supplies. Central Asian military cooperation is still at a very early stage, but an important step was taken when, in May 1996, the Kazakh, Kyrgyz and Uzbek defence ministers agreed on the creation of a joint peacekeeping force of 500 men under UN auspices.[18]

The Central Asian states have tried to create confidence and establish stability through regional cooperation. In January 1997 the presidents of Kazakhstan, Kyrgyzstan and Uzbekistan signed a treaty of 'eternal friendship' in which they undertook not to allow their territories to be used for armed aggression or any other activities hostile to their co-signatories. Nazarbayev commented: 'These documents say that in the event of any problems arising in interstate relations, between the ministries and government departments of the three states, in border areas or for our peoples … a commission should be set up to solve the issues.' The most substantial threat to stability in the wider Central Asian region is Afghanistan. Turkmenistan, Kyrgyzstan and Kazakhstan have proposed arranging an international conference and inviting the Afghan parties to the conflict to attend, together with representatives of several states with an interest in the region.

[15] As reported in January 1997, the trilateral union plays a role in developing the countries' economies. Trade turnover between them increased by 60 per cent over the past two years and at the end of 1996 commercial operations with Kazakhstan and Uzbekistan accounted for about 50 per cent of Kyrgyzstan's foreign trade. *Inside Central Asia,* no. 154, 6–12 January 1997, p. 6.

[16] *Inside Central Asia,* no. 115, 1–7 April 1996, p. 3.

[17] Russian agencies, 12, 15, 16 December 1997; Jamestown Foundation, *Monitor,* vol. 3, no. 237, 19 December 1997

[18] Each republic provides approximately the same number of servicemen who will be stationed in the south Kazakhstan region on the border with Uzbekistan. *Inside Central Asia,* no. 119, 29 April–5 May 1996, p. 6.

11

The CAU thus provides a common platform for the Central Asian states in strengthening their role in relation to Russia and to the outside world. The support of the two largest countries of Central Asia is an important factor for success. Uzbekistan and Kazakhstan are often viewed as competitors for the role of regional leader, which might create future tensions within the organization. Uzbekistan, with its large ethnic minorities in Tajikistan and Kyrgyzstan, is also watched warily by its neighbours who suspect it of nourishing plans for expanding its influence in Central Asia. Uzbekistan denies any such plans, and has instead concentrated on developing cooperation with its neighbours. So far the CAU seems to be serving as an important structure constraining its members from developing eventual tendencies to acquire disproportionate power, and thereby maintaining stability in the region.

The new international network

The new network of international relations that is rapidly developing in Central Asia reflects not only the efforts by these states to reach out to the outside world, but also a much wider international interest in these countries which were once more or less isolated from direct international contacts as republics of the Soviet Union, landlocked and without their own direct communication lines to the outside world. The new network of international relations is strongest in the economic field of trade, investment and transport, and also in the military and security field.

Foreign capital from Europe, America and Asia is being invested in all Central Asian states. By mid-1997 Kazakhstan had the fifth largest cumulative foreign direct investment value among all post-communist countries, in per-capita terms ranking second only to Hungary. Foreign capital is finding its way to the strategic sectors of metallurgy and oil and gas.[19] As agreements are being signed with foreign companies, the Central Asian leaders stress that they strike deals with whoever offers the best commercial conditions.[20]

Trade is expanding with neighbouring non-CIS countries and also with countries further afield. Trade statistics cannot be fully relied on, as not all trade is recorded. They do, however, indicate the shifting patterns in the region, with new partners playing an ever-increasing role. An example is Kazakhstan's growing trade relations with the European Union and especially with Britain, Germany and Italy.[21] In 1997 the European Union's share of Kazakhstan's total exports constituted 26.8 per cent

[19] *Kazakhstan Country Commercial Guide* (CCG), Ch. 10 – appendices. *BISNIS* (Business Information Service for the Newly Independent States), home page (http://www.iep.doc.gov/bisnis/bisnis.html), February 1998.
[20] Interview with Kazakhstan's foreign minister Tokayev in *Nezavisimaya gazeta*, 18 September 1997, p. 3.
[21] *Kazakhstan Economic Trends*, Quarterly Issue, January–March 1998 (TACIS).

compared with 17.9 per cent in 1996, while its share of Kazakhstan's total imports amounted to 21.6 per cent in 1997 compared with 13 per cent in 1996.[22]

China is a growing market for Central Asia, especially for Kyrgyzstan and Kazakhstan.[23] In 1996 China rose from third to second place in terms of its share of overall Kazakh exports, with raw materials and technical equipment constituting a high percentage of the total. In 1995 China was Kyrgyzstan's fifth largest trading partner with 16.5 per cent of its total exports. By 1997 China had become Kyrgyzstan's largest trading partner, with an estimated 30 per cent share of its total trade.

Of crucial importance is the extension of railways and roads that connect the Central Asian states with their neighbours to the east and to the south. The rail extensions into China and Iran are parts of a much larger attempt to overcome geographical obstacles. There are ambitious plans for modernizing and extending existing railway systems to link Europe and Asia, by a 'Trans-Asian Railway' from the port of Lianyungang on the Yellow Sea in the east, to the port of Rotterdam in the west (via Urumchi, Almaty, Tashkent, Ashgabat, Istanbul and Budapest).[24] This proposal forms a part of a larger transportation and energy corridor made up of interlocking railways, ferries, pipelines, and communication systems. The rail connections with Iran via Mashhad–Serakhs–Tedzhen and with China over Druzhba form part of this corridor. A north and south rail connection is also being prepared. In May 1996 the presidents of Kazakhstan, Turkmenistan and Iran signed a memorandum on the construction of a link from Mangyshlyak on the Caspian coast in Kazakhstan to Iran across Turkmenistan. This would connect the whole of the former Soviet railway system, stretching all the way to Murmansk in the north, with the Persian Gulf.[25] These long-term projects would also open up possibilities for Russia as they would become the shortest routes across the continents. There are EU-supported plans to connect the three Caucasian states and the five Central Asian states by the development of a 'Eurasian Transport Corridor' (TRACECA). In the spring of 1996 Azerbaijan, Turkmenistan, Georgia and Uzbekistan signed an agreement on the construction of a railway connecting Chardzhou (in Turkmenistan) with Turkmenbashi, Baku (across the Caspian), Tbilisi and Poti/Batumi (in Georgia).[26]

---

[22] This trend was maintained during spring 1998.

[23] *Kazakhstan Economic Trends*, January–March 1998 (TACIS).

[24] I. S. Zonn, *Kaspiiskii memorandum (vvedenie v geopoliticheskoe kaspivedenie)*, Moscow, Russian Academy of Natural Sciences, 1997, p. 116. Compare Peter Sinnott who writes that in October 1994 an agreement was signed between China, Russia and the five Central Asian states to improve the effectiveness of the railway known as the 'Second Eurasian Continental Bridge'. Peter Sinnott, 'Central Asia's Geographic Moment', *Central Asia Monitor*, 1997, no. 4.

[25] Zonn, *Kaspiiskii memorandum*, pp. 121–2.

[26] Ibid., p. 123.

Kyrgyzstan and Bulgaria have joined the project, and Ukraine and Kazakhstan have shown an interest in joining.[27]

The increased cooperation within Central Asia coincides with similar efforts between other CIS states apart from Russia. Ukraine and Georgia have been active in developing relations with Central Asia. To both these states the issue of energy deliveries along alternative routes to the traditional Russian ones has become central. The prospect of Kazakh and Azeri oil being transported via Georgia therefore opens new opportunities. In November 1997 the regional association GUAM was created, consisting of Georgia, Ukraine, Azerbaijan and Moldova. The guidelines of the new alliance included the development of the Eurasian and Transcaucasian corridor projects and work towards integration with European and Atlantic structures.[28]

In Central Asia's efforts to expand trade and commerce Iran plays a significant role as a transit country to foreign markets. Primarily it assists its neighbour Turkmenistan, but it also provides Uzbekistan with surface transport privileges for lorries carrying cotton for export overseas. Kazakhstan has been able to export oil through a swap arrangement, whereby Kazakhstani crude oil is delivered to Iran's Caspian ports and equivalent quantities of Iranian oil are exported via the Persian Gulf on Kazakhstan's behalf.[29]

A broader interest by the Central Asians to join organizations whose member states are culturally and linguistically close was reflected in their 1992 membership of the Economic Cooperation Organization (ECO), comprising the Muslim states of Afghanistan, Iran, Pakistan and Turkey. ECO's aims are to develop regional projects in energy production, transport and communications, and in the creation of trade and economic infrastructures.

Among the countries now playing a pivotal role in Central Asia is the United States. In 1997 US Deputy Secretary of State Strobe Talbott declared the whole of the Caucasus and Central Asia to be of strategic interest to the USA. This corresponds well with Central Asian efforts to diversify foreign relations. All the Central Asian states appear to share the Kazakh foreign minister Tokayev's words that

> we think that the US should be present in Central Asia, since in any region of the world it is desirable to see a functional system of balance and mutual checks. Yes, we give priority to our relations with Russia, China and other neighbouring states. At the same time we are interested in having the American presence strengthened in the region.[30]

---

[27] Ukraine definitely plans to join, and Kazakhstan has expressed its interest. The project is important for Uzbekistan; currently more than 50 per cent of all Uzbek freight crosses Russian territory.
[28] *Inside Central Asia*, no. 200, 24–30 November 1997, p. 6.
[29] Jan S. Adams, 'The CIS States: going global', *CSIS Post-Soviet Prospects*, vol. V, no. 1, March 1997.
[30] Kazakhstan's foreign minister Tokayev in an interview in *Nezavisimaya gazeta*, 18 September 1997, p. 3.

In 1992 the Central Asian states became members of the United Nations and the Conference on Security and Cooperation in Europe (in 1995 renamed the Organization for Security and Cooperation in Europe, OSCE), thereby gaining direct access to a much wider international network than the CIS can provide on security and on humanitarian and economic affairs. As a consequence Central Asian government circles, at least, are becoming more exposed to the international community.

With regard to military issues, too, the Central Asian states are searching for wider international structures and the means of decreasing their dependence on Russia. All of them except Tajikistan became members of NATO's Partnership for Peace programme in 1996. September 1997 witnessed the first exercise of the newly created joint Kazakh–Kyrgyz–Uzbek peacekeeping battalion within the framework of the Partnership for Peace programme. More than 400 American soldiers participated, together with token units from several countries, among them Russia. Roza Otunbayeva, then Kyrgyzstan's foreign minister, said that the formation of the battalion was proof that the Central Asian states were looking at non-CIS options for 'reliable guarantees of national security'.[31]

The Central Asian countries have also demonstrated an interest in developing military cooperation with other states. Officers are sent for military training in non-neighbouring states, among them the USA. Reflecting the new interest in diversifying military cooperation, the Kyrgyz Defence Minister Subanov declared in June 1997 that Kyrgyzstan was seeking broader military cooperation with China, and stressed that this would become 'one of Kyrgyzstan's foreign-policy priorities'.[32]

A new network of international relations is evolving as the Central Asian states try to diversify their foreign relations. A new political map of cooperation is thus developing on former Soviet territory beyond Russian control, with sub-groupings being created and contacts and exchange schemes developing with non-neighbouring countries. Russian commentators have described this as a process of 'Russia being gradually squeezed out of Central Asia, economically as well as military-politically'.[33]

[31] *Novaya gazeta*, 14 February 1996; Roger D. Kangas, 'With an Eye on Russia, Central Asian Militaries Practice Cooperation', *Transition*, 9 August 1996.
[32] *Inside Central Asia*, no. 177, 16–22 June 1997, p. 3.
[33] Mekhman Gafarly, 'Tsentralnoaziatskii soyuz prevrashchetsya v voennyi blok', *Nezavisimaya gazeta*, 20 December 1997, p. 3.

3 RUSSIA IN SEARCH OF A POLICY TOWARDS CENTRAL ASIA

What does Central Asia mean to Russia?

The driving force underlying Russian expansion in Central Asia in the mid- and late nineteenth century had been military considerations, and the overriding factor was a desire to challenge the British empire along the Asian periphery.[1] The Curzon Line became the dividing line between the Russian and British spheres of interest, and later the border of Soviet Central Asia to the south. The Soviet leaders inherited a view of Central Asia as being of great military and geo-strategic significance to Russia and to the Soviet Union. The first function of Central Asia was to provide a barrier, on the southern edge of the Eurasian heartland, to any attack from the south; the second was to shore up the vulnerable lifeline connecting the eastern and western extremities of the empire.[2]

Since Russia had conquered Central Asia, the latter was regarded as an integral part of the Russian empire. Yet from the beginning there was a duality in the Russian approach to the region. Its value lay mainly in its geographical location but it remained alien because of its different religion, culture and traditions. This duality was also reflected in Russia's ideological self-perceptions. Russia understood itself as being culturally close to Asia but also as having a 'civilizing' role and mission there.

At the time of the break-up of the Soviet Union, Central Asia had come to be regarded mainly as an economic burden on a stagnating Soviet economy. In 1990 Alexander Solzhenitsyn advised Soviet leaders to concentrate on developing the Slavic heartland and to more or less turn their back on Central Asia. The perception of Central Asia as a burden, as well as a culturally, spiritually and politically alien territory, was confirmed by its initial exclusion when the three Slavic republics took the initiative in creating the Commonwealth of Independent States in early December 1991.[3]

[1] Milan Hauner, *What is Asia to Us? Russia's Asian Heartland Yesterday and Today*, London and New York, Routledge, 1992, pp. 44–5.
[2] Ibid., p. 115.
[3] Eugene B. Rumer, 'Russia and Central Asia After the Soviet Collapse', in Jed C. Snyder, ed., *After Empire*, p. 49 (see above, Chapter 2, note 1).

To Russia's economic reformers at the time of the break-up of the Soviet Union, Central Asia was not significant for any military or security considerations, and its geographical location was of no importance. Since the time of Gorbachev, the reform debate had concentrated on a Russian withdrawal from all costly obligations outside Russian territory.

The break-up of the Soviet Union inflicted a heavy blow on Russia's relations with Central Asia. A new basis for the relationship had to be created, and a search for a policy was initiated. The answer to the question as to what would be the most expedient policy became dependent on Russian domestic politics, influenced by competing interests. Just as there has been no common understanding of what Russia is and what its national interests are, so there has been no common understanding of what Central Asia means to Russia, or what Russia's policy towards the region ought to be.

Of the Central Asian states Kazakhstan continued to be regarded as highly important to Russia's interests, owing to the long common border and its large Russian population. Already in August 1992 the unofficial but politically influential Council on Foreign and Defence Policy, in its document 'A Strategy for Russia', advised the Russian government to concentrate on relations with Kazakhstan, Belarus and Georgia as countries of key interest.[4]

Main directions of policy

Russia's search for a policy towards Central Asia after the break-up of the Soviet Union roughly follows its search for a policy towards the CIS in general.

Neither the Russian government of 1992 nor its Foreign Ministry under Andrei Kozyrev was successful in formulating a novel policy towards the newly independent states. The main preoccupation of Kozyrev at that time was relations with the West; the complex issues of relations with the new states that now occupied former Soviet territory were often avoided or postponed. As a result, Russian policy towards Central Asia during 1991–2 can best be characterized as 'withdrawal and confusion'.[5]

From 1993 to 1995 a second period can be discerned, which may best be described as years of 'great-power rhetoric'. Statements during 1993 by President Yeltsin and his Foreign Minister Kozyrev reflected a turn in policy towards what was called 'the near abroad'. Russia's fear of losing its influence over the former Soviet territories to more distant powers which would, as Kozyrev said, 'fill the power vacuum' became of overriding concern. The government thereby paved the

[4] 'Strategiya dlya Rossii', *Nezavisimaya gazeta*, 19 August 1992, pp. 4–5.
[5] For an overview of the search for a new foreign policy during the first year of independence, see Lena Jonson, 'Russia in Search of a Nationalist Interest: The Foreign Policy Debate in Russia', *The Nationalities Paper,* vol. 2, no. 1 (spring), 1994.

way for the new consensus on foreign policy shared also by a wider group of politicians, who only a year earlier had been considered hardline nationalists. This consensus included a determination to regain great-power status, to dominate former Soviet territories, and to deny all non-CIS states a foothold in this region. Thus Russia was once more embracing its tradition of a *'zero-sum perspective'* in understanding Central Asia.

Russia became more concerned with the new threats to its security brought about by the break-up of the Soviet Union. Fear of the likely consequences to Russian security from armed conflicts in the newly independent states was already reflected in the May 1992 draft of the Russian military doctrine. Such conflicts were considered a threat to Russian security and to its internal stability.[6] The Tajik civil war which erupted in the spring of 1992 helped to shape Russian perceptions of a Muslim threat spreading into Central Asia and into Russia's own Muslim heartland. As Russia was left with new and permeable state borders, it became more concerned with the problems of smuggling, drug-trafficking and illegal trespassing across borders. The answer to these problems was sought in a geo-political strategy towards the CIS and towards Central Asia in general. Once again Central Asia gained importance to Moscow for security reasons.

The new foreign policy consensus of 1993 also brought about a shift in the perception of Russia's relations with the West, namely that its interests may coincide or partly overlap with the latter but never be identical to them. However, to this was also added larger Russian concern with the competitive aspects of international politics. A report by the Russian Foreign Intelligence Service under its then head, Yevgenii Primakov, emphasized the threat of Western and Muslim governments trying to advance their influence on the former Soviet territories.[7] The threat to the Central Asian states, notably Tajikistan and Uzbekistan, posed by the turmoil in Afghanistan was thus viewed from the perspective of out-of-region states increasing their influence by exploiting the crises and instability of the former Soviet territories.

In 1993 Russian official statements with regard to the former Soviet territories became more militant, as did Russian policy. As Russia was not capable of continuing an active and interventionist policy, a gap developed between its ambitions and capability, and between its rhetoric and actual behaviour. Russian policy in the war in Tajikistan in 1993–5 illustrates this growing gap. What started as its support for one side taking power in the Tajik civil war developed into full Russian support for a regime completely dependent on assistance for its survival,

---

[6] See the draft of the military doctrine published in *Voennaya mysl* (special edition), no. 4–5, May 1992.
[7] 'Rossiya – SNG: Nuzhdaetsya li v korrektirovke pozitsiya Zapada?', *Rossiiskaya gazeta*, 22 September 1994.

and into Russian involvement in a civil war. Several factors explain Russia's change of policy in the Tajik civil war in 1996, but the growing realization that Russia did not have the resources or the capability for military victory played an important part. The Chechenia war of 1994–6 made the military and political leadership aware of Russia's weakness. The consequence for policy in Tajikistan was an appreciation not only that the Tajik conflict could not be won by military means, but also that interference by Russia ran the risk of undermining its position in the whole of Central Asia. This resulted in strong Russian pressure for a political accommodation between the Tajik parties to the conflict and ultimately to their signing of a political accord in June 1997.

Thus, a third period in Russia's policy on the former Soviet territories was initiated in 1996. It can be described as a 'pragmatic search' for solutions to problems on CIS territory. It involved political accommodation between the parties in conflict, and a 'wait and see' approach to efforts to integrate former Soviet territories. The new foreign minister Yevgenii Primakov (appointed in January 1996) represented this more pragmatic trend. Yet he was appointed with the support of wider groups within the Russian establishment as someone determined in his efforts to defend and promote Russian state interests. His policy change evolved within the 'zero-sum perspective' but reflected an awareness of the existing restrictions on Russian capability.

Yeltsin's election victory in 1996 for a second term as president and the appointment of the 'young reformers', Anatolii Chubais and Boris Nemtsov, in March 1997, strengthened a growing trend towards a more economic-oriented strategy on the CIS as a whole. The new government confirmed the priority given to Russia's own economic growth and economic reforms, but showed an awareness of new economic opportunities to the south and east of Russia. Boris Nemtsov, until December 1997 the minister responsible for oil, gas and electricity, helped pave the way for energy agreements with both Turkey and China in 1997. The government thereby reflected the growth of Russian business interests beyond the country's borders and in the Central Asian states themselves.

Yet, so far Russia's search for a policy towards Central Asia remains within a 'zero-sum perspective', from which it watches the changing political scene in Central Asia and the growing network of international relations with anxiety. A 'cooperative perspective' remains no more than an option for the future.

Foreign policy strategies, means and levers

When Russian efforts at integration intensified in 1993, Moscow followed a *political strategy*. When the Russian government became more concerned with strategic aspects of its future role in Central Asia and in the CIS, it tried to promote economic as well as military integration. This was considered crucial in order to keep the new states united under Russian leadership, to stop foreign influence in countries close to Russian borders, and to rebuild Russia's international status as a great power.

To formulate a policy on integration the Russian government had, however, to decide what price it was prepared to pay for the integration of the former Soviet territories. Yeltsin's words in February 1994 reflect the dilemma of combining the wish for integration and leadership with efforts to avoid all obligations that might be costly or harmful to Russia's own economic development: 'Integration must not bring harm to Russia itself or lead to over-stretch of our forces and resources, material as well as financial'.[8] As no solution to this dilemma was found, the government remained uncertain as to what economic benefits integration might bring to Russia.

A second question was how to promote integration among independent states. Russia had opted for both bilateral and multilateral integration. Bilateral agreements came to play a more significant role as multilateral attempts by the CIS at integration stalled. With regard to multilateral cooperation, Russia had only vague ideas about how to proceed.

In the spring of 1993 Yeltsin had suggested a step-by-step process of integrating CIS territories along the lines of European Community integration.[9] As no economic mechanisms were found to stimulate and encourage integration, political means were tried instead. Political decisions prescribing economic integration were taken at CIS summits, but new decisions could not be implemented. Owing to strong suspicion among the non-Russian CIS member states towards integration and towards any centralized supra-state structures, the CIS remained a loose organization without executive powers or control mechanisms.[10] Within Russia strong criticism was raised from the very start against the organizational structure of the CIS.

---

[8] *Rossiiskaya gazeta*, 24 February 1994.

[9] Mark Webber, *CIS Integration Trends: Russia and the Former Soviet South*, London, RIIA, 1997.

[10] In principle CIS statutes demand consensus for decisions to be made, but in practice they allow a member to abstain from voting and to be excluded from the decision-making process. They also accept national revisions of the phrasing of the decision through the addition or removal of parts of the text as the national parliament ratifies the document. Hundreds of decisions and resolutions have been adopted by the CIS but very few have ever been implemented.

Russia remained committed to its objective of an integrated post-Soviet territory but without knowing how to proceed. Yeltsin's decree of September 1995 'On Russian strategy towards CIS member states' declared the ideal of the creation of an economic, political and defence union but without giving any idea of how it was to be achieved.

As integration did not develop, the Russian government opted for a differentiated policy with regard to the CIS. In 1995 Russia created a CIS Customs Union with Kazakhstan and Belarus alone, joined by Kyrgyzstan in early 1996. In spring 1996, just before the Russian presidential election, the four states signed an agreement on 'deeper economic integration', while Russia and Belarus signed a symbolic treaty of union. The new integration structures of such a 'mini-CIS', hastily proclaimed, gave the impression not only of a desperate search for results but also of yet another effort to initiate integration by proclamations from above. Such an approach was criticized in a document by the Council on Foreign and Defence Policy in 1996. In its May 1996 document, 'Will the Union be restored? Prospects for post-Soviet space', a strategy was suggested whereby cooperation was to be initiated and encouraged from below rather than from the top.

The October 1997 CIS Summit in Chisinau was interpreted by many commentators as a watershed in CIS history and the beginning of the end of the organization.[11] Criticism of the CIS as an organization and of Russian policy had been heard before, but not so outspoken. The CIS presidents left without signing any of the documents prepared for the summit. Moscow at first did not admit the seriousness of the situation, mainly reporting Yeltsin's criticism of the CIS as inefficient and inadequate. However, as pointed out in the Russian media, the inefficiency of the CIS stemmed more from a lack of political will among its leaders than from the CIS statutes. There were many signs that the CIS had reached the ultimate crisis point.[12] Since then the CIS Summit, which it was announced would discuss fundamental reform of the CIS, has been repeatedly postponed.

From 1993 to 1995, as CIS economic integration efforts failed, military cooperation was given greater emphasis in spite of Russian official statements that the former was to have a central role. Military agreements appeared more easy to implement and therefore more effective in binding the states together. Already in 1992–3 Moscow signed bilateral friendship and cooperation treaties with all the Central Asian states, actively taking upon itself military obligations to end conflicts on CIS territory in the hope that a multilateral defence organization would develop.

[11] Jamestown Foundation, *Monitor*, vol. 3, no. 209, 7 November 1997.
[12] Yet there is an important aspect of the CIS framework and institutional structure that should not be overlooked. With its meetings and summits it provides a forum for discussions on issues of joint Russian and Central Asian interest.

As such engagements became too costly, it had to cut military spending both inside and outside Russia.

Yet in the policy debate the option of military integration remained. Its supporters became more vocal in 1996 against the background of what was perceived as a threat to Russia's western flank resulting from the enlargement of NATO, and to its southern flank from increased penetration by other countries. The proposed enlargement of NATO increased Russian official rhetoric about the need to close ranks on CIS territory and to create a CIS defence alliance. Military integration was recommended by several voices in the government and in public debate. It was seen as the answer not only to NATO enlargement but also to what was perceived as an anti-Russian alliance developing from Ukraine through Georgia and Azerbaijan into Central Asia and Uzbekistan. As Moscow saw the geopolitical map of Central Asia changing at an increasing rate, voices critical of the government's Central Asia policy were heard.

In December 1996 Defence Minister Igor Rodionov again proposed the creation of a CIS defence union and the pooling of CIS military forces.[13] His speech at a conference of the Staff of the Council on Military Coordination of the CIS carried the title 'Strategic interests of the CIS member states' and was interpreted as a hardline approach. He claimed that Western states constituted an external threat through their efforts to split the CIS, to prevent Russia gaining strength, and their plans to use the wealth of Central Asian natural resources to the benefit of the West. Rodionov's speech echoed voices from within the Russian military demanding that military integration be given priority as the core of all integration efforts. This was followed in the spring and summer of 1997 by unsuccessful Russian proposals to promote military integration within the CIS.

To others in the Russian debate, military integration did not seem feasible and would therefore fail to secure Russian influence. Evidently, other kinds of levers had to be found. The Council on Foreign and Defence Policy, in its May 1996 document 'Will the Union be restored?', emphasized the argument that Russia could no longer rely on military means to exert power, but had to turn to economic levers for influence.[14] The phrase already coined in an earlier document from 1994 was applied once more: 'leadership instead of control, economic dominance instead of political responsibility'. The authors of the document argued that only an economically strong Russia would attract the new states of the former Soviet territories and be able to counter the growing influence of foreign states.

[13] Igor Korotchenko, 'Igor Rodionov vystupil za sozdanie oboronnogo soyuza stran SNG', *Nezavisimaya gazeta*, 26 December 1996, p. 1.
[14] 'Vozroditsya li soyuz?', *Nezavisimaya gazeta*, 23 May 1996.

The importance of restoring an economic network of relations where the old Soviet one had fallen apart was stressed in government statements, but no tools to initiate it were found. The need for Russian capital investment in Central Asia and in other CIS countries was emphasized by official representatives.[15] However, as this was not followed by appropriate government measures, nothing happened. Investments for political reasons were hardly attractive to Russian speculators, who had doubts about investing even in Russia itself.[16] In the Russian media debate demands were made for the government to support and encourage investment in Central Asia.

An economic strategy within a zero-sum perspective would lead to different outcomes from one within a cooperative perspective. While the latter would only try to promote business interests, the former would use economic levers to maintain a dominant role.

The Russian government came to view energy as an important lever in integrating the CIS and in May 1995 Yeltsin issued a decree setting out long-term Russian energy strategy to the year 2010.[17] Though general in content, this was the first official document to indicate a foreign policy-related role for the oil and gas industry.[18] Yeltsin approved a new long-term energy strategy that defined the industry's major foreign economic goals as contributing to cooperation within CIS states, establishing a legal and economic environment to meet Russia's international agreements, and expanding cooperation with foreign countries to develop their energy resources and to acquire new energy markets for Russia's exports.[19]

In 1996 Primakov, pointing to the growing foreign interest in investing in Central Asia's infrastructure of transport and telecommunication, declared: 'Russia must become one of the most important partners to create new pipeline and railroad systems, satellite systems…'.[20]

A new emphasis on energy issues for the strategic control of Central Asia would help to pave the way for an economic strategy and provide Russia with the levers of influence to maintain its position as a regional power. The external orientation of

[15] See, for example, Yevgenii Primakov's presentation at the Council on Foreign and Defence Policy, *Nezavisimaya gazeta*, 17 March 1998.

[16] The need to invest for political reasons was reflected in the recommendation by the Institute of Foreign Economic Research of the Russian Academy of Sciences: 'It is important for the state to select regional and, when possible, country priorities for the development of economic relations. Their selection should be based on a complex evaluation of the opportunities and demands of the national economy and also on the geopolitical and economic significance for us of one region or another or the significance of the country.' 'Russia's Integration into the World Economy, Paths of Further Development of Russia's Foreign Economic Activity, *International Affairs* (Moscow), vol. 42, no. 5/6, 1996.

[17] *Rossiiskaya gazeta*, 16 May 1995.

[18] Igor Khripunov and Mary M. Matthews, 'Russia's Oil and Gas Interest Group and its Foreign Policy Agenda', *Problems of Post-Communism*, vol. 43, no. 3, May/June 1996, p. 41.

[19] Ibid.

[20] 'Soveshchanie poslov Rossii v stranakh SNG', *Diplomaticheskii vestnik*, no. 9, September 1996.

the oil and gas conglomerate aligns it with the main thrust of Russia's foreign policy on the integration of former Soviet territories, though this congruence is perhaps more coincidental than deliberate. '[T]o credit the Russian government with manipulating the oil and gas complex for achieving its foreign policy objectives would be a gross overestimation of its current potential.'[21] Whether the new interest and lobby groups in Russian foreign policy-making will act together with the government or whether their interests will clash is yet to be seen.

Russia's potential willingness to revert to its long tradition of coercion to promote its interests and influence states beyond its borders has been widely debated among its neighbours. Historically this includes not only the use or threat of violence and economic sanctions and blackmail in order to put pressure on states and governments, but also direct measures to destabilize the domestic climate within the countries concerned. In 1993 such means were used by the government structures in order to force states back into the Russian orbit. Russia's economic and military weakness since then has undermined the use of traditional great-power levers and methods, but such an option is still present in the media debate. Today, few would publicly recommend such measures for Russian policy towards the CIS countries; Konstantin Zatulin, director of the Moscow-based Institute of the CIS, and the publicist Andranik Migranyan are exceptions.[22]

The fear of Russian use of coercive means to destabilize them is very active among CIS states, and, predictably, there was a strong reaction among CIS leaders when Zatulin and Migranyan's highly controversial manifesto appeared in the Russian media just before the CIS Summit in March 1997. Foreign Minister

---

[21] Khripunov and Matthews, 'Russia's Oil and Gas Interest Group', p. 46.

[22] In their manifesto of March 1997 they asserted: 'Only active measures (right up to destabilization of the domestic political situation in regions) can stop the process of disintegration.' They recommended fuelling contradictions within the Central Asian elite, and stirring up a conflictual atmosphere with the help of the Russian-speaking minority. They also advised the Russian government to concentrate on loosening the Central Asian bloc of states, splitting it up and strengthening intra-regional rivalry, and suggested that Moscow, with the use of 'carrot and stick' techniques, would force the Central Asians to accept concessions and change their leadership. The 'stick', they suggested, would include limiting ('regulating') exports of raw materials from Central Asia over Russian territory and the use of Russian transport infrastructure, as well as severe conditions for restructuring Central Asian debts to Russia. 'SNG: nachalo ili konets istorii?', *Nezavisimaya gazeta*, 26 March 1997. In December 1997, they again argued: 'To our mind, only coercive impulses (*silovye impulsy*) can today drastically change the relations of the post-Soviet Asian republics with Russia ... In spite of a growing anti-Russian direction in the politics of these countries, they themselves have such an explosive domestic potential. If Russia would concentrate its efforts on some of these directions, these states would rapidly have to face the choice: to become friendly with Russia or to completely cease to exist.' 'SNG posle Kishineva. Nachalo kontsa istorii', *Sodruzhestvo NG* (supplement to *Nezavisimaya gazeta*). no. 1, 2 December 1997. See also the article on Kazakhstan by Aleksandra Dokuchaeva, Andrei Grozin, Konstantin Zatulin, 'Respublika Kazakhstan i interesy Rossii', *Nezavisimaya gazeta tsenari*, no. 8, 10 July 1997, pp. 5–6.

Primakov had to declare publicly that such views did not in any sense reflect the policy of the Russian government. Nazarbayev expressed his nation's fear when in a June 1997 interview on Kazakh TV he warned that Kazakhstan must be prepared to defend its independence against forces in Russia which might otherwise bring it back under Russia's control. He said there were no problems in relations with the present Russian authorities, but that the improving situation in Kazakhstan and the continuing problems in Russia might encourage those forces to seek to undermine Kazakhstan's sovereignty.

> Today [Russian] policy [towards Kazakhstan] is all right, and thank God everything is fine with our neighbours! But what if tomorrow some radical comes to power in Russia and says that he will restore the Soviet Union: 'Join us in the way Belarus has done or in some other way, or else we will make you join by force.' The programme of the ill-wishers includes: 'First, Kazakhstan's economy must be suppressed and not allowed access to external markets. Second, Kazakhstan must be made to quarrel with its neighbours, with Uzbekistan in particular. If we make them quarrel they both will weaken and come to us for help.' Thus, they want to create a situation similar to that in Tajikistan. 'Third: Let us spread speculation about head of state Nazarbayev... If that does not work, there is the last way: to stir up ethnic Russians living in Kazakhstan with the idea of separatism and set them against ethnic Kazakhs.'[23]

There is a continuing shift in favour of an economic strategy but still within a zero-sum perspective. An economic strategy within a 'cooperative perspective' remains only a vague option for future government policy. However, as commercial interests and independent groups develop, they add new dimensions to Russia's external relations.

Policy-making and foreign policy actors

Russian foreign policy-making in the first half of the 1990s has been characterized as chaotic and politically deeply divided.[24] This is especially true with regard to policy towards the countries of the former Soviet Union. With the dissolution of central authority after the break-up of the Soviet Union no clear decision-making procedure could be discerned.[25] The Russian president and parliament were stuck in a tug of war and the old Soviet-Russian constitution was of no help in authorizing a

---

[23] *Inside Central Asia*, no. 178, 23–29 June 1997, p. 4.
[24] Scott Parrish, 'Chaos in Foreign-Policy Decision-Making', *Transition*, 17 May 1996.
[25] Neil Malcolm et al., *Internal Factors in Russian Foreign Policy*, London/New York, RIIA/Oxford University Press, 1996.

division of power between the branches. This situation lasted up to the autumn of 1993. In October that year Yeltsin had a showdown with parliament and in December a new constitution was adopted which increased the power of the president to the detriment of parliament. During these years a groundswell of political forces initiated policies for which the Russian government had to carry the responsibility. In 1992 and 1993 local Russian military forces in the Caucasus and Tajikistan had intervened in the evolving conflicts. The Russian military thus came to play an important role in shaping foreign policy towards the new states of the former Soviet Union.

Though the 1993 constitution had increased presidential power and weakened parliament's role in foreign policy-making, a situation of fragmentation continued.[26] The Foreign Ministry lacked authority in relation to other ministries and institutions. The military remained strong in spite of interdepartmental rivalries. The media continued to carry articles complaining about the lack of a coordinated foreign policy. Yeltsin alternated between two remedies: either declaring that the Foreign Ministry had the authority to coordinate all foreign policy actions, as was the case in the decrees of November 1992 and March 1995; or forming an interdepartmental body for that purpose, as happened in December 1992 and December 1995.[27]

When Yevgenii Primakov became foreign minister in January 1996, the Foreign Ministry was able to assert its influence, and the power of the military was reduced. The reason was, however, not only the change of foreign ministers. Equally important were the structural changes taking place as a consequence of the cutback in the military budget, which reduced the capability and influence of the armed forces in foreign policy.

The collapse of the communist system and the transition to a market economy paved the way for economic interests groups to play a role in policy-making. New independent or semi-independent players emerged, competing for influence over national policy.[28] In 1995 the Russian specialist Yuri Fedorov discerned four main lobby groups in foreign policy. These were 'the new market forces' including commercial banks and other financial facilities, as well as companies involved in trade and services; the military-industrial complex and high-technology industries; the oil and gas industries; and the agricultural sector and commodity producers. Fedorov observed that the political influence of producers of raw materials in general, and of the oil and gas sector in particular, had become especially important

[26] Scott Parrish, 'Chaos in Foreign Policy Decision-Making'.
[27] Ibid.
[28] Yuri Fedorov, *Economic Interests and Lobbies in the Formulation of Russian Foreign Policy*, Post-Soviet Business Forum Briefing no. 5, London, RIIA, June 1995.

as this sector was the major source of Russian hard-currency earnings. He concluded that 'oil and gas interests are becoming an important factor in Russia's "carrot and stick" policy in the "near abroad", which seeks to exercise strategic control over areas that are critical to the production and transportation of major exports.'[29]

Fedorov described the policy-making situation as one in which the president and his entourage decided the most important strategic outlines of foreign and security policy, while governmental agencies exercised considerable independence in implementing the directives. Lobby groups were largely concentrated in the government and neither the president nor his 'inner cabinet' could afford to ignore the interests of the dominant economic and military elites.[30]

To what extent do the interests of the oil and gas industry overlap with those of the government? There is a duality in the status of these industries, some of which are partly state-owned or state-controlled. As pointed out in one Western study of the Russian oil and gas industry, 'Gazprom is a government agent managing the country's single gas monopoly and, therefore, cannot be a purely commercial business. On the other hand, Gazprom is becoming an independent economic actor, approaching the development of the Russian gas market exclusively from the point of view of corporate gain'.[31] The same can be said about the oil companies, even though they are mainly privatized.

Other economic interests have also increased their influence in Russian domestic and foreign policy. These relate to a large degree to the important role adopted by the banks and bank-led financial-industrial groups (so-called FIGs) in the last few years. The explosion in number and influence of FIGs in Russia is a new phenomenon. They did not develop until 1992–3 and they are controlled by private banks.[32] The result of this process is that a few banks have incorporated enterprises into their FIGs, which join together the biggest private banks in Russia with many of Russia's largest industrial enterprises. Bank-led FIG holdings in oil in 1997 included Menatep/Rosprom (YUKOS); LogoVAZ (Sibneft); and ONEKSIMbank/Interros (Sidanko). Gazprom and Lukoil, on the other hand, created and control three powerful banks: the Imperial Bank, the National Reserve Bank and Gazprombank.[33]

The bank-led conglomerates have become significant actors in Russian policy-making. As owners of media empires and with the financial means to fund election

---

[29] Ibid.
[30] Ibid.
[31] Khripunov and Matthews, 'Russia's Oil and Gas Interest Group', p. 40.
[32] Juliet Johnson, 'Russia's Emerging Financial-Industrial Groups', *Post-Soviet Affairs*, vol. 13, no. 4, 1997, pp. 333–65. See also Valery Kryukov and Arild Moe, *The Changing Role of Banks in the Russian Oil Sector*, London, RIIA, 1998.
[33] Johnson, 'Russia's Emerging Financial-Industrial Groups', pp. 334 and 346–7. The deep economic crisis erupting in August 1998 had a serious impact on the banks. The Imperial Bank immediately went bankrupt.

campaigns they were important to Yeltsin in his re-election campaign of 1996. Bankers today move freely from their commercial offices to government service and back. Boris Berezovskii from LogoVAZ is one example. In 1997 he became a Deputy Secretary of the Russian Security Council, and in April 1998 he was appointed Secretary of the CIS. The methods whereby policies are made have thus changed as new interest and lobby groups have emerged in Russia.

The Russian regions have also strengthened their position and have assumed greater independence from the Russian state. On the local level, authorities, companies and organizations are actively developing contacts with their counter-parts in other countries. As a consequence they have personally established direct contacts with the regions in Central Asia, particularly along the Russia–Kazakhstan border.

The new political landscape in Central Asia is systematically undermining Russia's traditional means of exerting power and influence. As the Central Asian states consciously try to reduce their dependence on Russia and diversify their foreign contacts, Russia loses levers for influencing them. Since 1993 the Russian government has become clearer on general objectives in Central Asia, but no consistent government policy yet exists. As a result of a fragmented policy-making situation where interest and lobby groups play a larger role, Russian government structures have simultaneously pursued different policies. However, developing common interests between economic groups and the government are leading to a more economic orientation of Russian strategy in Central Asia.

4 MILITARY ISSUES

Threats and perceptions of threat

At the time of the break-up of the Soviet Union the Russian leadership initially tried to maintain joint military forces of the CIS, and a Joint Military Command was created. However, as the trend to build up national armies was much stronger among the new states, the former Soviet forces soon broke up into smaller national entities. This trend was as strong in Russia as in the other states, and President Yeltsin in a decree in May 1992 declared that a Russian national force would be set up. In the summer of 1993 the Joint Military Command was dissolved and replaced by a Joint Military Coordinating Council.

Initially, Russia was able to offer considerable guarantees to the Central Asian states with regard to their domestic and external security. With little military experience and few military officers and trained personnel, these states had looked to Russia for assistance to build up their national military forces. In 1992 and 1993 Russia was successful in signing bilateral agreements on military cooperation with individual CIS countries. Initially all Central Asian states except Turkmenistan also joined multilateral agreements on military cooperation.

The embryo of a joint defence organization was created as early as May 1992 in the form of the Tashkent Treaty of Collective Security. The Tashkent Treaty, which is mainly concerned with external threats, commits the signatories to refrain from the use of force against one another and to consult one another on all important security matters. At that time only six states signed the treaty, but a further three did so a year later. All the Central Asian states except Turkmenistan became signatories. However, military integration did not follow and the Tashkent Treaty remained a paper policy.

The draft of the Russian military doctrine published in May 1992 referred to the threat of 'local wars'. However, the main threat to security did not emanate from conflicts between states but from within them. The Tajik civil war that erupted in the spring of 1992 caused Russia further concern about security threats. The Tajik war also played an important role in changing Russian priorities on intervention in armed conflicts on former Soviet territory and in the military integration of CIS territories. In September 1993 Russia managed to persuade Kazakhstan, Uzbekistan and Kyrgyzstan to agree to the establishment of a CIS peacekeeping force in Tajikistan. The troops the Central Asians sent were only a token force while the largest number of troops were supplied by Russia. The Tajik conflict thus initiated a military cooperation which Russia wanted to extend into a much broader and deeper military integration. However, the Central Asian states remained reluctant to accept this. They also resisted all efforts to develop any permanent peacekeeping mechanisms.

Russian policy in handling the Tajik conflict, which in 1992–3 had had the support of Uzbekistan, in 1995 evoked strong criticism from the presidents of that country and Kazakhstan. Disagreement developed between Kazakhstan and Uzbekistan on the one hand and Tajikistan and Russia on the other over what Nazarbayev and Karimov regarded as the Tajik President Rakhmonov's unwillingness to find a compromise with the United Tajik Opposition. The risk of a rift developing was one of the factors behind Russia's change of policy on the Tajik conflict in 1996.[1]

The Central Asian leaders initially shared Russia's perception of the 'Islamic threat', preferring a development model that was secular in orientation. President Karimov, fearing a fate similar to the dismissal of President Nabiyev in Tajikistan in 1992, supported Russia in its intervention in the turmoil there, assisting the Popular Front to install Rakhmonov in power in the autumn of 1992. However, evaluations of what exactly constituted the 'Islamic threat' came to vary.

Russia perceived the sources of the threat as both external and internal. The external sources were seen as emanating specifically from the south – that is, Iran, Afghanistan and the Middle East. In this context Central Asia in 1993 had become a security concern by being Russia's 'soft underbelly'. Andrei Kozyrev and the so-called 'Atlanticists' in the Russian policy debate drew no distinctions between different political forces within Islam. Kozyrev stressed that Russia had common interests with the West in restraining the Islamic threat.[2] A 1994 report by the Russian Foreign Intelligence Service, headed by Primakov, stressed the distinction between 'Islamic fundamentalism' and 'Islamic extremism', pointing out that only the latter was dangerous. This distinction paved the way for more sophisticated political analyses and became official policy after Primakov became foreign minister.

Afghanistan is regarded by Russia as a main source of instability, thereby threatening Russia's southern flank. The Taliban take-over of Kabul in September 1996 gave Russia a new impetus to achieve military integration in Central Asia. In February 1997 as the situation in Afghanistan deteriorated, Yeltsin met with Defence Minister Rodionov and the Head of the Russian Federal Border Troops,

[1] Lena Jonson, *The Tajik War: A Challenge to Russian Policy*, Discussion Paper 74, London, RIIA, 1998.
[2] Mohiaddin Mesbahi, 'Russia and the Geopolitics of the Muslim South', in Mohiaddin Mesbahi, ed., *Central Asia and the Caucasus after the Soviet Union*, Gainesville, FL, University Press of Florida, 1995.

Andrei Nikolayev, to discuss what could be done 'to prevent a military-political catastrophe' if the war should reach the southern borders of the CIS.[3] On Yeltsin's instruction Nikolayev conducted intensive negotiations aimed at creating an effective collective security system in the south and a mechanism for localizing conflicts as far away as possible from Russia's own borders.[4] Yet the outcome of Russia's efforts was not integration, but merely increased cooperation with the Kyrgyz authorities on border defence. Immediately after the Taliban take-over in Afghanistan, Turkmenistan chose to stay out of all CIS summits and discussions on joint measures concerning the new situation to the south, thereby clearly reflecting the diverging perceptions of the main security threats both within the region and in relation to Russia.

In February 1995, Russia managed to get all the Central Asian states except Turkmenistan to sign a document outlining collective security. This document presented the main concepts of a joint security system,[5] but it was already evident that the perceptions of external security threats had started to diverge. To Russia such threats are the impetus for military integration. Yeltsin urges that more attention be paid to 'ensuring security and developing military cooperation' to counter attempts to establish centres of power in former Soviet territories. He declared that 'we have no interest in seeing the former Union's territory dominated by anyone, particularly in the politico-military sphere, or in seeing any country playing a role of buffer against Russia'.[6]

The Central Asian states view it differently, and this can also be seen with regard to NATO and its enlargement to the east. President Karimov has declared that he is not against the extension of NATO. Kazakhstan, with its closer military cooperation with Russia, cautiously stresses the need to take Russian interests into consideration. Yet in its military doctrine it calls for a 'military-political union with the Russian Federation simultaneously with close cooperation with NATO aimed at Kazakhstan's membership in the Alliance' as a condition necessary for security.[7] In the spring of 1998 Kazakhstan was the first Central Asian state to open a permanent mission at NATO's headquarters.

In 1998, against the background of events in Afghanistan, Russia, Uzbekistan and Tajikistan decided to coordinate their struggle against religious extremism.

[3] Y. Golotyuk, 'Afghan War Becomes Threat No. One to Russia', *Segodnya*, 22 February 1997, p. 3.
[4] A. Zhilin, 'Russia's Border Coincides with Turkmenia', *Moscow News*, 8–15 June 1997, p. 9.
[5] 'Kontseptsiya Kollektivnoi bezopasnosti gosudarstv–uchastnikov dogovora', *Diplomaticheskii vestnik*, no. 3, March 1995, pp. 34–7.
[6] *Krasnaya zvezda*, 8 October 1996. Quoted by Roy Allison, 'The Network of New Security Policy Relations in Eurasia', in Roy Allison and Christoph Bluth, eds, *Security Dilemmas in Russia and Eurasia*. London, RIIA, 1998, p. 27 (n. 2).
[7] A. Grozin and V. Khlyupin, *Nezavisimoe voennoe obozvenie*, no. 23, 28 June–4 July 1997, pp. 1 and 3.

However, this political alliance was mainly motivated by the Uzbek and Tajik leaders' concern about domestic opposition in general. It did not make Uzbekistan more positive with regard to military cooperation with Russia.

For the Central Asians the main threats to security are not so much external as internal. The real threat, according to the Kazakhstani security expert Oumirserik Kasenov, is 'the danger of "Afghanization"', that is 'the possibility of the new Central Asian states cracking at their seams, as is occurring in Afghanistan'.[8] The threats to security as described by President Karimov in his book published in 1997 are also mainly internal, emanating from, among other factors, regional and inter-ethnic conflicts, religious extremism, crime and corruption.[9]

However, there is a common threat perceived by Russia and by the Central Asian states – the fissiparous borders which are open to smuggling, drug-trafficking and an inflow of illegal migrants. The unprotected borders are open also to the inflow of refugees, a matter which became of major concern to the Central Asian states, notably Kyrgyzstan, as the war in Afghanistan intensified in 1996–7, forcing Russian, Kazakh and Kyrgyz border troops to conduct joint military exercises.[10] This is the kind of threat that in future will surely encourage cooperation but not necessarily result in military integration.

Bilateral cooperation

In 1992 all the Central Asian states signed bilateral treaties with Russia on 'friendship, cooperation and mutual assistance', by which they are obliged to render each other military assistance in the event of aggression against either party. Kazakhstan was the first Central Asian signatory. The two sides agreed that they would form a 'united military and strategic zone and jointly use the military bases, test sites and other military infrastructures'.[11] The treaty was considered by Yeltsin and Nazarbayev to be a model for all Central Asian states. In 1994 these treaties were followed by further treaties on military cooperation.[12]

But even though Kazakhstan had from the outset included close cooperation with Russia as a key element in its military doctrine, plans for a 'common defence space'

---

[8] Oumirserik Kasenov, 'Central Asia: National, Regional and Global Aspects of Security', in Allison and Bluth, eds, *Security Dilemmas in Russia and Eurasia*, p. 190.

[9] Islam Karimov, *Uzbekistan on the Threshold of the Twenty-first Century*, London, Curzon, 1997.

[10] *Nezavisimaya gazeta*, 5 May 1997, p. 3.

[11] Itar-Tass, 25 May 1992.

[12] In January 1995 an agreement was signed by creating a joint group of Russian and Kazakh troops, which would operate 'on the principles of joint planning for the training and use of troops' (Allison and Bluth, eds, *Security Dilemmas in Russia and Eurasia*, p. 20). See also Martha Brill Olcott, *Central Asia's New States: Independence, Foreign Policy and Regional Security*, Washington, DC, US Institute of Peace Press, 1996, p. 70.

did not materialize and military cooperation stagnated. At the time of the visit by the Russian Defence Minister Sergeev to Almaty in October 1997, his ministry was of the opinion that Russia's military cooperation with Kazakhstan was quite inadequate.[13]

Given the long common border, cooperation over air defence was considered highly important, and joint Russian–Kazakh patrols started in the early summer of 1996. Anti-aircraft defence remains an area of close cooperation and was singled out as such by the Kazakh defence minister in October 1997.[14] Russian border troops assist in guarding the 1,700 kilometres of border with China in a development of so-called joint Russian–Kazakh operational forces. A national Kazakh border troop service was set up in 1993, and cooperates closely with Russian border troops. With the normalization of relations with China as a result of the September 1996 border agreement between Russia, the Central Asian states and China, the need for a Russian presence will decrease.

There are several issues in dispute between the two countries. Among them is the Baikonur cosmodrome, site of all the former Soviet Union's space launches. Russia has the right to lease Baikonur on a contract for twenty years,[15] but has reneged on its payments.

The long common border remains another issue of dispute. Because it is almost completely unguarded it provides easy access into Russia for drugs, smuggling and those seeking illegal entry. The cost of border installations is considered too high, but unarmed Cossack volunteer units were introduced in March 1997 on an experimental basis in four Russian border regions – Saratov, Orenburg, Chelyabinsk and Omsk. After a trial period such units were to be extended to cover the whole joint border.[16]

However, Kazakhstan's foreign ministry severely criticized this decision as constituting 'a breach of existing agreements on border patrol procedures'.[17] In September 1997 the head of the Russian Border Troops Service, Andrei Nikolayev, visited Kazakhstan and a border accord was signed. The experiment with Cossack units was not abandoned. Nikolayev gave an assurance that 'no informal units will guard the border', promising that Russia would formalize and regularize the participation of units such as the Cossacks in guarding its borders. Nazarbayev also obtained a vague promise that Russia would cooperate with Kazakhstan in 'gradually beginning' the work of border delimitation and 'in preparing and signing at a

[13] Andrei Korbut, 'Vizit Igorya Sergeeva v Kazakhstane', *Nezavisimaya gazeta*, 28 October 1997, p. 3.
[14] RFE/RL Newsline, no. 133, 7 October 1997.
[15] Baikonur also houses testing facilities for liquid-fuelled ballistic missiles. Martha Brill Olcott, *Central Asia's New States*, p. 71.
[16] *Inside Central Asia*, no. 165, 24–30 March 1997, p. 4.
[17] Reported by Kazakh TV, 16 April 1997; *Inside Central Asia*, no. 168, 14–20 April 1997, p. 4.

future time' a border treaty.[18] The border between Russia and Kazakhstan has yet to be demarcated or regulated.

Kazakh efforts to participate in wider international cooperation are also reflected in military issues. Agreements on military cooperation with other countries have been signed, among them one with China in the autumn of 1997. In January 1996 Russia undertook to assist Kazakhstan in creating a national coastguard in the Caspian Sea, but as it was unable to deliver any vessels, Kazakhstan has accepted ships from other countries.[19]

Uzbekistan's close military cooperation with Russia in the early 1990s made Western experts believe that this would develop into a 'pillar of security in Central Asia' and provide 'the military arm of a Russian–Uzbek political consensus in the region'.[20] However, this did not happen. Instead, Uzbekistan developed into one of the staunchest critics of multilateral CIS military integration. It has created the strongest military force in Central Asia, with an army of reportedly 70,000 men, and is determined to build up a national defence force independent of Russia.[21] There are no Russian troops and no Russian military objects on Uzbek territory. At the beginning of 1995 an air squadron of MiG-25s, which was the last part of the CIS peacekeeping force stationed in Uzbekistan, was redeployed to Tajikistan.[22] Uzbekistan is the only Central Asian country that has not signed an agreement allowing Russian citizens to do military service in its national army.

On the two most important issues to Russia – border protection and air defence – Uzbekistan has reduced its cooperation with Russia since 1995. No Russian border guards are deployed on the frontier with Afghanistan, though the two countries cooperate on border issues. The agreement of 28 March 1997 is one example of such cooperation, which does not imply any closer collaboration.[23] On the issue of air defence Uzbekistan and Russia have signed a bilateral agreement, which mainly implies an exchange of information.[24] According to the Russian Air Defence Commander, the

[18] Jamestown Foundation, *Monitor*, vol. 3, no. 182, 1 October 1997.
[19] Agreement was reached on Russian aid to create a Kazakhstani Caspian flotilla (Kasaev in *Nezavisimaya gazeta*, 31 January 1996, p. 1). See also 'Voennaya delegatsiya Rossii v Kazakhstane', *Nezavisimaya gazeta*, 27 January 1996, p. 1. Russia was to give five ships for this purpose and Russian specialists were to explore the coastal infrastructure of Kazakhstan. Alexander Pelts and Anatoly Ladin, 'In Alma-Ata the foundation was laid for the development for military cooperation', *Krasnaya zvezda*, 30 January 1996, p. 1; *FSU 15 Nations: Policy and Security*, January 1996, p. 23.
[20] Mohiaddin Mesbahi, 'Russia and the Geopolitics of the Muslim South', p. 289.
[21] *Obshchaya gazeta*, 20–26 June 1996, p. 5; *FSU 15 Nations: Policy and Security*, June 1996, p. 94.
[22] Andrei Krotov, 'Sensatsiya v Dushanbe', *Nezavisimaya gazeta*, 31 October 1996, p. 3.
[23] The agreement covers cooperation in border protection, exchange of information and prevention of terrorism, drug and arms smuggling, illegal border-crossing, etc. and also efforts to ensure the security of Russian and Uzbek borders with non-CIS states. *Inside Central Asia*, no. 165, 24–30 March 1997, p. 3.
[24] A bilateral agreement on further air defence cooperation was signed by Russia's Air Defence Commander General Viktor Prudnikov on a visit to Uzbekistan in late summer 1997. *Nezavisimaya gazeta*, 25 October 1997, p. 3.

Uzbek anti-aircraft missiles and radar facilities are in good condition. The two countries are cooperating to supply new equipment and maintain the existing fleet of aircraft.[25] However, as Uzbekistan is distancing itself militarily from Russia, old military equipment is being replaced by the United States instead of Russia.

Turkmenistan, situated far from Russia and sharing a long border with Iran, has gradually reduced its security dependence on Russia. Its 1992 treaty with Russia was unique as it envisioned the formation of a national army under joint command.[26] The air force and air defence systems came entirely under Russian control. Logistics, training and exercise were in Russian hands, but Turkmenistan shared the costs. However, Turkmenistan's political desire to become independent, and its declared neutrality, made it reduce its cooperation with Russia.[27] A national Turkmen army was set up and there are no longer any Russian military troops on active duty on Turkmen territory.[28] In 1995, the 1992 agreement on military cooperation, which among other things had provided for Russian bases in Turkmenistan, was annulled. Turkmenistan did not sign the CIS air defence treaty of 1995 but demanded instead the withdrawal of Russian anti-aircraft and air forces from its territory.[29]

Turkmenistan's status as a 'neutral' state was recognized by the UN General Assembly in December 1995. As a demonstration of its neutrality and its attitude towards CIS military cooperation, Turkmenistan only sends 'observers' to CIS meetings to discuss joint security measures. In September 1996 the 1994 Turkmen military doctrine was amended to underline the country's neutral status. It declares that Turkmenistan 'does not take part in any military blocs, alliances or interstate association involving rigid mutual obligations or providing for collective responsibility of members; ... shall not allow foreign military bases on its territory'. However, it 'shall take part in world community efforts designed to prevent wars and armed conflicts and in peacekeeping efforts'.[30]

With regard to Turkmenistan's southern borders, in August 1992 an agreement was signed between Turkmenistan and Russia on the joint protection of the Turkmen border and on the status of Russian border troops in Turkmenistan. Since 1993 a unit of Russian border troops has been deployed on the Turkmen–Afghan

---

[25] Uzbekistan has a regiment of Su-27 fighters. General Prudnikov in *Kommersant-daily*, 11 April 1996; *FSU 15 Nations: Policy and Security*, April 1996, p. 28.

[26] Mohiaddin Mesbahi, 'Russia and the Geopolitics of the Muslim South', p. 290.

[27] Ibid. p. 291.

[28] *SWB* SU 2280 S1/ 4–5.

[29] A bilateral agreement on air defence cooperation was reported in the Russian media to have been signed in the late summer of 1997. Andrei Korbut, 'Naznachenie', *Nezavisimaya gazeta*, 25 October 1997, p. 3.

[30] *Neutral Turkmenistan*, 2 October 1996; *FSU 15 Nations: Policy and Security*, October 1996, p. 93; *Inside Central Asia*, no. 141, 30 September–6 October 1996, p. 3.

frontier, and in 1995 it was reorganized into an 'Operational Group of Russian Border Troops' to assist the newly established national Turkmen Border Troops.[31] However, in November 1996, shortly after the Taliban take-over of Kabul, Nikolayev signed an accord with the Turkmen border authorities in Ashgabat on the reduction of Russian troops guarding Turkmenistan's southern borders.

As a result of Turkmenistan's interest in diversifying its foreign relations and becoming part of wider international networks, it has stated its willingness to participate in the Partnership for Peace Programme and has set out plans for such cooperation up to 1999. In the bilateral programme of August 1997 Turkmenistan pledged to participate in joint exercises as an observer and in the training of officers.[32]

Both Kyrgyzstan and Tajikistan are small and vulnerable. Kyrgyzstan is situated between large neighbours and Tajikistan is torn apart by civil war; both depend on Russia for their military security. This is especially true of the Rakhmonov regime which has been completely dependent on Russian support. Their permeable borders are considered a problem for Russia.

In Kyrgyzstan there are no longer any Russian military ground forces, only air defence units. Russian border guards remain, however, following the 1992 agreement whereby Russia assumes responsibility for defending the border with China.[33] In 1997 Kyrgyzstan decided to set up its own national border service which will gradually replace the Russian troops. As is the case in Tajikistan, a majority of the Russian border troops in Kyrgyzstan now consists of local inhabitants. Kyrgyzstan, fearing an influx of Tajik refugees at the end of 1996, enhanced its border cooperation with Russia and started a series of joint military exercises. In spite of its security dependence on Russia, Kyrgyzstan also shows signs of criticizing the military relationship. There have, for example, been accusations of Russian border troops being involved in drug-trafficking. President Akaev stated in autumn 1997 that 'Kyrgyz patience is not endless' and that 'Russian interests in Kyrgyzstan cannot be defended in a one-sided way'.

Tajikistan is a special case given the civil war from 1992 to 1997, in which Russia actively intervened in partisan support of one side. The intervention was carried out with the help of a former Soviet division, the 201st Motorized Rifle Division, and with Russian border troops. Such a strong Russian military presence turned Tajikistan into more of a protectorate than an independent state.

[31] Dianne L. Smith, 'Central Asian Militaries. Breaking Away from the Bear', *CSIS Post-Soviet Prospects*, vol. V, no. 7, December 1997.
[32] It also committed itself to maintaining civilian supervision over the armed forces and to take part in consultations to prevent and regulate political and military crises in Central Asia, and in joint environmental protection, communications and information systems programmes. *Inside Central Asia*, no. 186, 18–24 August 1997, p. 3.
[33] *FSU 15 Nations: Policy and Security*, September 1996, p. 49.

As a consequence of Russia's change of policy in Tajikistan in 1996, President Rakhmonov came under pressure to accept a political accommodation with the United Tajik Opposition (UTO). A National Reconciliation Commission started its work in September 1997 and a coalition government is to be created in which the UTO will be given 30 per cent of the posts. The UTO affirmed the importance of close relations with Russia. However, it is likely that if the peace process in Tajikistan continues the Russian military presence will be reduced, and that as Tajikistan seeks to diversify its external relations, including its military options, the bilateral relationship will become weaker.

Russia bears the brunt of the expenditure for the joint border guard service in Kyrgyzstan and Tajikistan.[34] Budget restraints are making it hard for Russia to maintain such a presence; however, in November 1997 it decided to cut its border troops in Tajikistan from 16,000 to 14,500. As it becomes more difficult to maintain a Russian presence in Central Asia and border protection cannot be expected to be carried out effectively, Russia has to strengthen its own national frontiers.[35]

Military cooperation within the CIS

The Tashkent Treaty on Collective Security was intended to be the embryo of a defence organization. In his September 1995 decree on Russia's relations with CIS states Yeltsin declared it to be Russian policy to create a system of collective security based on the Tashkent Treaty and bilateral agreements between Russia and individual CIS members. He stated that the Tashkent Treaty would develop into a defence union, that military infrastructure facilities would be preserved, the external borders of the CIS strengthened, the presence of Russian border troops in these countries guaranteed by mutual agreements, and joint efforts in peacekeeping operations secured. The decree sharply stated that CIS states would be obliged 'not to participate in any alliances and blocs directed against any of these states'.[36]

---

[34] In Tajikistan, the Russian share is said to be 50 per cent, and the rest to be paid by the Tajik government, which, however, is totally dependent on Russian support. In Kyrgyzstan Russia pays up to 80 per cent. The so-called operational groups in Kazakhstan and Turkmenistan are financed by Russia, while the borders and the border guard troops are provided for by these states. Andrei Nikolayev, 'Russia's Border Guarding Policy is Being Tested by Time', *Nezavisimoe voennoe obozrenie*, no. 17, 12 September 1996, pp. 1–2; *FSU 15 Nations: Policy and Security*, October 1996, pp. 51–2.

[35] Nikolayev explained this interest in the following way: 'We believe it is much more expedient to see to the interests of all CIS members along the former Soviet borders, and leave the internal borders open. But this should not be done at the expense of Russia's security. Hence, the "two borders" strategy our state currently follows.' Interview in 'A State Begins at its Border', *Krasnaya zvezda*, 6 February 1997, pp. 1–2. On the structure of Russia's Border Troops see ibid., pp. 37–9; *Vechernaya Moskva*, 2 October 1996, pp. 1–2.

[36] Decree by the Russian President on Russian strategy with regard to the members of the Commonwealth of Independent States, *Rossiiskaya gazeta*, 23 September 1995.

Nothing of this kind ever materialized. An integrative military structure has not been created.[37] Instead, Russia tried to initiate cooperation on a few selected issues, especially joint border defence, joint air defence and joint peacekeeping efforts. Even these specific issues have revealed the wider problems of trying to effect military integration.

In a September 1993 agreement Uzbekistan, Kazakhstan and Turkmenistan agreed to a CIS arrangement to strengthen the Afghan–Tajik border. Kazakhstan, Kyrgyzstan and Uzbekistan agreed to send a small number of border guards to join the Russian border troops. Yet they remained reluctant to get into a more formalized multilateral arrangement for a joint border protection system. At the May 1995 CIS Summit a general agreement on the protection of the outer CIS borders was adopted but failed to receive the signatures of five states, among them two Central Asian states, Turkmenistan and Uzbekistan. An agreement on exchange of information with regard to border issues was adopted in 1996 by seven states, but again Uzbekistan and Turkmenistan did not sign.[38] As no integrative border structures have been created, the functions of the CIS Council of Border Troop Commanders, which meets on a regular basis, are limited to matters related to arrangements at a regional level (particularly towards the situation in Tajikistan) and to bilateral contacts.

Russia continues to insist on the creation of a joint system for border protection as a way to stimulate military cooperation within the CIS. In May 1996 a document was signed on the cooperation of border troops in conflict situations along the external CIS borders; again Uzbekistan and Turkmenistan did not sign.[39] At the September 1997 meeting of CIS Border Guard Commanders Russia presented several draft documents on an integrative border regime which were turned down and sent back for 'further work'.[40] The drafts included documents on creating a

[37] The non-Russian CIS leaders showed their reluctance towards military integration by delaying decisions on drafts from one summit to another, or by not participating at all in decisions on CIS military cooperation. Opposition on military issues was seldom shown in public. Therefore the refusal to accept a Russian candidate to replace General Samsonov in the autumn of 1996 as Chief-of-Staff of the CIS Council on Military Coordination was something new. At the CIS Council of Defence Ministers meeting in Dushanbe in late October 1996 when the candidacy of Kolesnikov was refused, the opposition to him had said that this 'intergovernmental organization should be headed by a representative of some state other than Russia, because its citizens had already occupied this post' (Golotyuk in *Segodnya*, 31 October 1996, p. 1). Uzbekistan instigated Kolesnikov's rejection (*Nezavisimaya gazeta*, 31 October 1996, p. 3).

[38] 'Soglashenie ob obmene informatsiei po voprosam okhrany vneshnykh granits gosudarstv–uchastnikov SNG", *Diplomaticheskii vestnik*, no. 5, May 1966, pp. 34–6.

[39] 'Agreement on Cooperation of Border Troops of the CIS Member States in Conflict Situations along Outer Borders', *Diplomaticheskii vestnik*, no. 6, June 1996, pp. 42–4.

[40] As early as 1996 a draft on border troops in crisis situations was being discussed: *Nezavisimaya gazeta*, 20 December 1996.

single CIS border guard force to be used in crises on the external borders of the CIS and on turning CIS territory into a 'single border protection space'.[41] Turkmenistan did not even participate at the September 1997 meeting. Russia intended, according to Andrei Nikolayev, to have its border troops stationed in all CIS countries by the year 2001, and to create three Russian-led theatres of command for the border troops, one of which, the 'Southern', would have its centre in Tashkent.[42] These plans are highly unrealistic within the context of widespread reluctance about their implementation within the CIS.

The common interests of Russia and the Central Asian states mainly consist in cooperation with regard to the growing problems of smuggling, organized crime, drug-trafficking and illegal trespassing. Several agreements on practical cooperation to deal more effectively with these problems have been signed not only with regard to border troops but also between the Ministries of Interior Affairs and the security services.

Since February 1995 when Russia achieved agreement by all the Central Asian states (except Turkmenistan) on the intention to set up a unified CIS air defence system, not much has happened.[43] As a result of the agreement a CIS Air Defence Coordinating Committee was created, but no unified command structure followed, and no joint integrated air defence has been created.

All issues on the intervention of CIS peacekeeping troops or initiatives with regard to conflict resolution are to be formally decided by the heads of the member nations of the CIS. In reality peacekeeping policy is decided by Russia, but the formal CIS mandates are nowadays decided by the Council of Heads of States. Since this is a slow and complicated procedure, Russia has for a long time tried to create a common basis for approaching such issues. A conceptual document on conflict resolution and peacekeeping in the CIS was adopted in January 1996, and in March 1997 a decision in principle was taken to create a CIS Committee on Conflict Situations instigated by President Nazarbayev. Yet at the CIS Summit in Chisinau in October 1997 Nazarbayev, together with other CIS presidents, turned down the Russian proposal for what they saw as too much centralization of power in the Commission. According to Nazarbayev's proposal, the committee would comprise prime ministers and foreign ministers, and its task would be to study the situation in areas of tension and submit recommendations to the Heads of State.[44] Nazarbayev had become more outspoken in his criticism of Russia's interference in

[41] *Inside Central Asia*, no. 188, 1–7 September 1997, p. 2.
[42] The other two would be the 'Western' in Kiev and the 'Transcaucasian' in Tbilisi. Itar-Tass, 1–4 September 1997; Jamestown Foundation, *Monitor*, vol. 3, no. 165, 8 September 1997.
[43] *Diplomaticheskii vestnik*, no. 3, March 1995, p. 31.
[44] *Inside Central Asia*, no. 165, 24–30 March 1997, p. 4.

conflicts on CIS territory. In May 1997, in a sharply worded document, he accused Russia of being partisan in its supply of weapons in conflicts.[45]

To Russia a CIS Commission on Conflicts would be important not only to deal more efficiently with conflicts but also to provide a legal institutional framework for the mainly Russian interventions in situations of peacekeeping and conflict resolution. The Central Asians, on the other hand, shared the view of most of the CIS delegates that such issues would fall under the authority of the UN. This preference was clearly illustrated when Kazakhstan, Kyrgyzstan and Uzbekistan, in signing an agreement in May 1996 on the creation of a joint peacekeeping battalion, stressed that this battalion was to be used only under UN auspices.

In spite of the limited success in integration even on specific issues, the Russian government continued in its efforts to promote wider military integration. At the March CIS summit in 1997 a package of documents was presented on military-political and military-economic cooperation, suggesting an ambitious plan for military-political integration in three stages. The plan was not adopted. In spite of these continued efforts, there does not seem to be much optimism in Moscow concerning their outcome. Many people seem to share the opinion of the CIS Executive Secretary, Ivan Korotchenya, in February 1997 that 'the CIS countries have failed to show any progress in that sphere [military cooperation] over the past four years. Only recently were some structures formed, taking specific steps toward implementing the treaty.'[46] Moscow has to accept the sentiment spreading across Central Asia and expressed by President Karimov in his opposition towards the creation of any 'military-political blocs' on CIS territory. Military integration linking the Central Asian states to Russia is no longer an option.

[45] Aslan Kasaev, 'Nazarbayev vstretilsya s rossiiskimi zhurnalistami', *Nezavisimaya gazeta*, 17 May 1997, p. 3.
[46] S. Vorobiov, 'Time to Define Priorities', *Nezavisimaya gazeta*, 18 February 1997, p. 3; *FSU 15 Nations: Policy and Security*, February 1997.

5 THE CULTURAL SPHERE

A diminished Russian presence

At the time of the break-up of the Soviet Union the Russian population in Central Asia was about 9.5 million or 19.5 per cent of the total population. During Soviet times the Russian language was accorded privileged status and the Russian cultural heritage was safeguarded, albeit in a somewhat distorted Soviet form. Russians held a privileged position in society, and were well represented in senior positions in politics, administration and the sciences. Among the intelligentsia they constituted the majority in technical fields and in the pure sciences. The indigenous elite was raised within Soviet culture. It shared the same values and beliefs and was strongly secularized. All the Central Asian leaders who assumed power after independence were products of Soviet education and Soviet political life. The Kyrgyz president was the only one who had not followed a career in party politics. This constituted a strong cultural legacy that brought the Central Asian states close to Russia.

However, by the time of the break-up of the Soviet Union this pattern had already begun to change in three respects. First, the Russian population had started to leave for Russia; second, the indigenous elite had initiated a process of cultural nationalization; and, third, the Russian language had begun to lose its privileged position.

In the course of the nineteenth century, the first Russian settlers had arrived in Central Asia, in the wake of Russian troops. They came to play a major part in the development of agricultural production, irrigation, the expansion of arable land, building railways and towns, and the founding of heavy and mining industries. This was especially true for Kazakhstan. After the Second World War the influx of Russian immigrants to Central Asia continued, generated by extensive industrial development and housing construction, and by the campaign to recruit a workforce for the new industries.[1] In the 1970s the Russian population in Central Asia stopped growing as a result of a stream of Russians returning to their homeland. In the late 1980s the large number of Russian immigrants from Central Asia took the Gorbachev administration by surprise.

[1] Valery A. Tishkov, 'The Russians in Central Asia and Kazakhstan', in Yaacov Roí, ed., *Muslim Eurasia: Conflicting Legacies,* London, Frank Cass, 1995, pp. 290–91.

The Russian exodus had thus started well before independence. It was actually higher in 1990 than in 1991. However, after 1992 it rapidly increased and seemed to peak in 1995. During the following years it fell off, though remaining fairly high.[2] Over 60,000 people left Kazakhstan during the first eight months of 1997, compared with a total of 252,000 for the whole of 1994. Ethnic Russians comprised more than half of the migratory flow, ethnic Germans almost a quarter, and Ukrainians 8 per cent.[3]

There were various reasons for the early exodus. There were economic reasons. Several of the sectors where Russians dominated, such as the large industries, were heavily hit by the economic crisis.[4] Another factor which became important from the late 1980s onwards was the process of cultural awakening within Central Asian societies. As a result of this process, language laws had been adopted even before independence in all the Central Asian republics, strengthening the language of the titular nation.[5] Yet the language laws that were introduced prescribed a transition period of ten years to give people time to adapt to the new demands. The indigenous elite made nationalism, at this time prevalent mainly within the intelligentsia, part of its political platform. The new laws on citizenship, however, did not discriminate against the non-indigenous population, offering the possibility of becoming nationalized citizens to all those already resident in the country.

The Russian population felt marginalized. Outbreaks of ethnic violence, as in the Fergana valley in 1989, had contributed to a fear among Russians that they had no future in Central Asia, in spite of the fact that ethnic violence was never directed towards themselves. In 1996, Russian authorities reported that in total about a million immigrants per year had recently been arriving in Russia. The majority of them came from Central Asia. The 1996 Russian federal migration programme estimated that the influx of so-called forced migrants into Russia from other CIS countries would grow in the next few years to four million people, of whom 2.9 million would come from Central Asia.[6]

---

[2] During these years the Russians share of Kazakhstan's population dropped by 1 per cent to 36 per cent. The figure is deceptive since an average of 150,000 Russians per year have left Kazakhstan since 1990, and more than 75,000 Russians per year have arrived (mainly from other parts of Central Asia). Martha Brill Olcott, *Central Asia's New States: Interdependence, Foreign Policy and Regional Security*, Washington, DC, US Institute of Peace Press, 1996, p. 61.

[3] Reported by Tass, 19 September 1997; *Inside Central Asia*, no. 190, 15–21 September 1997, p. 4.

[4] Valery A. Tishkov, 'The Russians in Central Asia and Kazakhstan'. See also Neil Melvin, *Russians Beyond Russia: The Politics of National Identity*, London, RIIA, 1995; Paal Kolstoe, *Russians in the Former Soviet Republics*, London, Hurst, 1995.

[5] '… all of the local-language laws had been written before independence, with the intention of preserving and supporting local-language use in an environment dominated by Russian'. Martha Brill Olcott, 'Demographic Upheavals in Central Asia', *Orbis*, vol. 40, no. 4, Fall 1996.

[6] 'Iz federalnoi migratsionnoi programmy', *Diplomaticheskii vestnik*, no. 12, December 1996, p. 46.

The Russian population in Central Asia is thus declining. In 1989 Russians constituted 21.5 per cent of the Kyrgyz population, and in 1994 only 18 per cent. Between these years the Russian proportion of the population in Kazakhstan dropped by 2 per cent to 35.9 per cent. The average age of Russians remaining in Central Asia is much higher than that of the local population, and they constitute a disproportionately large number of pensioners.[7] Within the next decade or so, death from natural causes will be the main factor behind the decreasing number of Russians. The demographic composition of the population is thus undergoing a fundamental change.

One important consequence of this is that the cultural orientation of these states will also change. This affects Uzbekistan, Turkmenistan and Tajikistan in particular, since they share no border with Russia and have always had small Russian populations. The indigenous cultural heritage is being stressed. In Uzbekistan this has resulted in the rejection of all foreign influence and the promotion of a mythical Uzbek/Turkestani history and culture. In future, the Central Asian countries are likely to turn their attention southwards to countries with which they share closer cultural affinities, such as Turkey, Iran and Pakistan. As railways and roads are extended, new possibilities for contacts are developing. A similar process is taking place in Kazakhstan and Kyrgyzstan in their relationship with China.

The consequence of these processes will be that what was once a common cultural legacy will dissipate, and Russia and Central Asia will draw further apart.[8]

Russia's policy

The issue of Russian minorities on former Soviet territory became politically inflamed almost immediately after the break-up of the Soviet Union. It was used to define positions in a domestic Russian debate on national interest, and also to criticize Yeltsin and his government for selling out that interest.[9]

This partly explains why the defence of Russian minorities was given such attention in the draft of the Russian military doctrine published in May 1992. It became the responsibility of the Russian military to act in situations of 'violation of the rights of Russians outside the Russian Federation and of those who identify ethnically or culturally with Russia'.[10] The issue of the Russian diaspora remained central in Russian domestic politics and was reflected in Yeltsin's address to

---

[7] Martha Brill Olcott, 'Demographic Upheavals in Central Asia', p. 554.
[8] Cf. ibid., p. 555.
[9] Lena Jonson, 'Russia in Search of a National Interest: The Foreign Policy Debate in Russia', *Nationalities Paper*, vol. 22, no. 1, spring 1994.
[10] *Voennaya mysl*, 1992, no. 4–5, special edition.

parliament in February 1994: 'Dear compatriots! You are inseparable from us and we are inseparable from you. We were and will be together. On the basis of law and solidarity, we defend you and our common interests.'[11]

In November 1993 President Yeltsin issued a decree 'On the question of the protection of the rights of Russian citizens outside the Russian Federation'.[12] In connection with this the Russian Foreign Ministry was instructed to act more resolutely in the defence of the interests of Russian citizens abroad and to conclude bilateral treaties with the CIS states. The Russian government, however, did not express its concern for the Russian minorities either in military actions or in economic sanctions. Instead it tried to influence the governments concerned by turning the issue into one of international concern, mainly by referring to international law and norms.

The Russian government, fearing an influx of Russians from Central Asia, encouraged them to stay in the countries where they lived. Moreover, the Russian population was regarded as a bastion for Russian cultural influence in these countries.[13] In August 1996 a government programme was finalized following a presidential decree of August 1994.[14] The programme included five central policy objectives: creating legal conditions of respect for the rights of the Russian population in the countries concerned; giving financial and economic support to compatriots abroad; securing the use of the Russian language, and support for schools where the curriculum was taught in the Russian language; strengthening cultural links with Russia; and spreading information in Russian. At the same time a Federal Migration Programme was drafted on how Russia was to take care of the influx of 'forced migrants', as those were officially defined.[15]

However, the Russian government faced problems in implementing the programme as a result of budget restrictions. No money has been forthcoming to support the commercial activities of compatriots abroad. The number of Russian schools and the exchange of students have been cut. Other factors compound the problems of implementing the programme. Russian TV broadcasts have been reduced, partly owing to Russian's inability to pay the costs of transmission and partly owing to disputes with Central Asian governments on the broadcasting and transmission of programmes. As a result, in 1997 all transmissions of Russian programmes were temporarily suspended in Kyrgyzstan.

[11] *Rossiiskaya gazeta*, 25 February 1994.
[12] *Diplomaticheskii vestnik*, no. 1–2, January 1993, p. 8.
[13] See the document by the Council on Foreign and Defence Policy, 'Strategiya dlya Rossii', *Nezavisimaya gazeta*, 19 August 1992, p. 4–5.
[14] 'Programma mer po podderzhke sootechestvennikov za rubezhom', *Diplomaticheskii vestnik*, no. 6, June 1996, pp. 58–65.
[15] 'Iz federalnoi migratsionnoi programmy', *Diplomaticheskii vestnik*, no. 12, December 1996, pp. 43–50.

Cultural links with Russia are hampered by two additional factors which are beyond Russian control. First, other foreign TV channels are beginning to reach a Central Asian audience. Second, Russian journalists have been expelled from Central Asian countries when they have provided critical information on the domestic situation, especially in Uzbekistan. Nazarbayev has accused the Russian media of providing a distorted image of Central Asian societies.[16] Together, these factors contribute to the reduction of Russian cultural influence in Central Asia.

Russia tried to resolve the problem of the status and situation of Russians in the CIS countries by the introduction of dual citizenship. However, Moscow's demand that provision for dual citizenship be introduced there met with a mainly negative response. Most states regarded it as a blatant attempt to perpetuate the privileged status of Russians and a threat to their national sovereignty. In December 1993 Moscow signed the first treaty on dual citizenship with Turkmenistan, holding it up as a model for other states.[17] Concerned by the fact that its highly qualified Russian workforce was leaving the country, the Turkmen government had signed the treaty as an inducement to them to stay.[18] No other state has adopted dual citizenship legislation.

The legal position of the Russian population in the region is gradually being regulated. In spite of this, the issue remains a sensitive one and influences bilateral relations between Russia and the Central Asian countries, particularly Kazakhstan.

The large Russian population in Kazakhstan has obliged Nazarbayev to proceed carefully in order not to upset relations between the different nationalities within the population. In 1989, Kazakh was declared the state language of Kazakhstan. With Russians and other Europeans in almost exclusive control of high-level positions in important sectors of the Kazakh economy, the law was not to be implemented until the year 2010. Until then people without knowledge of the Kazakh language would be allowed to serve in official national posts. However, no law existed prescribing how to implement the declaration of Kazakh as the official language. In November 1996 Nazarbayev, well aware of the political sensitivity of the issue, endorsed a draft on language policy, sanctioning the status of Kazakh as the state language but at the same time granting Russian the status of a language of communication and integration within the CIS.[19]

Nevertheless, Russian reaction was forceful. In September 1996 the Committee on CIS Affairs of the Russian Duma issued a statement expressing concern at the

[16] Interview with Nazarbayev in *Nezavisimaya gazeta*, 16 January 1997, pp. 1 and 3.
[17] Leszek Buszynski, *Russian Foreign Policy after the Cold War*, Westport/London, Praeger, 1996, p. 101.
[18] To honour the agreement Yeltsin was awarded Turkmen citizenship.
[19] *Inside Central Asia*, no. 147, 11–17 November 1996, p. 4.

treatment of Kazakhstan's Russian-speaking population. It called on the Kazakh authorities to 'stop the persecution and harassment of the Russian population, and of Cossacks in particular', and demanded that the Russian president and government 'use all their powers to prevent the violation of generally accepted international norms in Kazakhstan'.[20] In May 1997 some members of the Russian government reacted strongly to the draft on language policy. Aman Tuleyev, then Russian Minister for Cooperation with CIS States, warned that there would be a massive exodus of Russian-speakers from Kazakhstan if the draft became law. He called for the revision of the provisions in the draft giving priority to the Kazakh language over Russian, claiming that they contradicted the principles of the Treaty on Friendship and Cooperation between Russia and Kazakhstan of 25 May 1992.[21] Prime Minister Chernomyrdin had to intervene to repair the damage to Russian–Kazakh relations caused by Tuleyev. Shortly after this Tuleyev was sacked.

Nazarbayev asked the Constitutional Court of Kazakhstan to rule on whether the law complied with the constitution of Kazakhstan. In July 1997 a modified version of the draft was published and the new law was adopted. This gives Kazakh the status of official language but strengthens the status of the Russian language relative to the draft, declaring it to be 'officially used on a par with the Kazakh language in state organizations and bodies of local self-government'.[22] Thus political compromise was found. Issues of citizenship and the legal rights of Russian citizens permanently living in Kazakhstan were also resolved during 1997.[23]

In spite of this progress with regard to the legal situation of the Russian population, the issue of their status and situation remained inflammatory in Russian–Kazakh bilateral relations. As parts of the Russian population in Kazakhstan became politically active in opposition to the Kazakh government, they found moral support among politicians in Moscow. The so-called patriotic bloc created in February 1997 by more than 150 ethnic Russian and Cossack organizations in

[20] *Inside Central Asia*, no. 139, 16–22 September 1996, p. 4.
[21] *Inside Central Asia*, no. 148, 18–24 November 1996, p. 4.
[22] *Inside Central Asia*, no. 181, 14– 20 July 1997, p. 4.
[23] *Inside Central Asia*, no. 182, 21–27 July 1997, p. 4. The law on citizenship in Kazakhstan followed the 'zero principle', granting citizenship to everyone living in the country. However, for those who asked for Russian citizenship but chose to live in Kazakhstan the legal situation remained to be regulated. In January 1995 an agreement was signed between Yeltsin and Nazarbayev making it easier for an individual to be granted citizenship and the legal rights of a citizen. The agreement also allowed the right to own property to people who chose Russian citizenship but continued to live in Kazakhstan. In talks with Nazarbayev in November 1996 Yeltsin proposed an agreement on the status of ethnic Russians living in Kazakhstan, defining their personal guarantees and the status of the Russian language. In July 1997 the bilateral agreements signed by Yeltsin and Nazarbayev in January 1995 regulating issues on citizenship and residence finally came into force. See also the interview with the Kazakh Foreign Minister Tokayev in *Nezavisimaya gazeta*, 18 September 1997, p. 3; *Inside Central Asia*, no. 149, 25 November–1 December 1996, p. 4.

Kazakhstan in defence of their rights is an example. The new political bloc urged the Russian leadership to carry out a linkage policy between Russia's offer of economic and political cooperation with Kazakhstan and Kazakhstan's observance of respect for the rights of its ethnic Russians.[24]

Russian cultural influence in Central Asia is waning. The long-term trend points to a decreasing share of Russians in the total population of the Central Asian countries. In spite of the Russian government's declared will to encourage the Russian population to remain in Central Asia it does not have the financial or economic means to support them or make it attractive for them to stay on. For the time being Russian remains the lingua franca in the region. Educated people in these countries still know and use the language. How long this situation will continue if Russian is not supported by the Central Asian governments as a common language remains to be seen.

[24] *Inside Central Asia*, no. 160, 17–23 February 1997, p. 4.

6 ECONOMIC RELATIONS AND TRANSPORT SYSTEMS

A common network?

The Soviet republics had been bound together in a joint system of production relations, communications and internal trade, which was shattered when the Soviet Union collapsed. The new states are all rebuilding their own national economies internally. However, these states have several problems in common. First, they share the same heritage of a centralized state economic system, and they are all to varying degrees introducing market reforms. They are also all part of the once common production structure with its inbuilt division of labour and common infrastructure of electricity grids and railways. This common legacy may in some respects be viewed as an asset to promote cooperation, but it can also be regarded a burden and a cause of dependency on Russia. It is such dependency from which the Central Asians are trying to free themselves.

Today there are two contrasting trends with different sets of dynamics. At the national level there is a continuing reduction of interdependence between Russia and the Central Asian states. At the local level new forms of cross-border cooperation and interdependence are developing.

Kazakhstan, more than any other Central Asian state, was closely linked to Russia, and its northeastern region was more closely integrated with Siberia and the Russian Federation than with the rest of Kazakhstan.[1] Close integration of industrial plants, a single energy system, and railway and road networks made this territory into a unified system in spite of administrative borders. New state borders led to the disintegration of this system, with disastrous consequences for the economy. However, this situation started a process of reorientation, and new forms of cross-border cooperation were initiated by local leaders and developed between regions along the border between Kazakhstan and Russia. This phenomenon is significant as it shows a way forward for the development of the common economic legacy, to the benefit of all parties.

The trend towards a reduced interdependence at the national level is reflected in the reorientation of trade away from Russia. Several factors explain this trend. It

[1] Neil Melvin, 'Southern Siberia and North-east Kazakhstan: Relations Along the Eurasian Border', paper presented at conference on Russia's regions, Carnegie Moscow Center, Moscow, January 1998.

48

may be regarded as a natural process of trade diversification after the restrictive Soviet trade and border regime had been removed. To some extent it can be explained by the introduction of national customs and trade regimes. Most importantly, however, the Central Asian states today can buy more cheaply on world markets than from Russia.

A crucial factor in the diversification of Central Asian economic relations is the increased possibility for communication with the outside world. In the past, the main obstacle had been the Central Asian infrastructure, the legacy of the Soviet system whereby Moscow constituted the hub and contact of every kind with the outside world had to pass across Russian territory. Consequently, the Central Asian states now give priority to the construction of a more diversified infrastructure. Since independence national airlines have been set up and national airports modernized, so that there are flights to more destinations than ever before.[2] Roads and railways are being extended across state borders. Grandiose schemes have appeared, promising to cut distances and find connections and outlets to remote ports and foreign markets. However, with limited financial resources the realization of some projects will be postponed well into the future.

The issue of railways gives an apt illustration of the problems inherent in a common economic legacy, but also of the grandiose visions for the future nourished by the Central Asians. After the break-up of the Soviet Union, the Central Asian states were landlocked, without transport extensions to shipping points outside the Soviet grid. The basic rail system linking Central Asia with European Russia and Siberia was built in the late nineteenth century. There were few connections, however, across the border to neighbouring countries. The main connections from Central Asia were either via the Trans-Siberian railway, north of Lake Baikal, or via the Trans-Baikal and East Siberian railway, south of the lake.[3] International traffic was given low priority in the Soviet era, and the link between China and Kazakhstan, on which work had commenced in the late 1950s, was not completed until 1992. Before 1992 goods and passengers had to be transferred between railheads by road at the border points. Today the whole of the former Soviet railway system is in need of repair, and transport tariffs have increased, making the use of Russian railways costly for the Central Asian states.

Since independence, new connections have opened linking the Central Asian states to the outside world. To the east, a connection with container handling and gauge transfer facilities and links to the Trans-Russian railway was opened in 1992

---

[2] The large new airport of Ashgabat is a good example.

[3] Gavan McDonell, *The Euro-Asian Corridor: Freight and Transport for Central Asia and the Caspian Region*, Post-Soviet Business Forum, London, RIIA, 1995, pp. 15–21.

between Druzhba in Kazakhstan and Urumchi in China's Xinjiang region.[4] To the west, the Turk-Sib line, running through Central Asia from Turkmenbashi in Turkmenistan, has been linked to Baku by a frequent roll-on/roll-off ferry and other shipping services.[5] To the south, the twin towns of Serakhs in Turkmenistan and Sarakhs in Iran were connected in May 1996, thereby linking Turkmenistan to the Iranian rail network. The link to Iran involved completing and modernizing a rail link between Tedjen in Turkmenistan and Mashhad in Iran.[6]

All railway plans and projects reflect a strong political will in Central Asia to diversify contacts with the outside world. Reorienting the transport infrastructure is one of the most difficult tasks. Many of these projects are costly, however, and it will take time to find the money to realize them. In the meantime national railway systems are being connected by shorter links. Together with new roads these are contributing to the creation of a new network of routes for commerce. This network opens new options for transport for Russia too, by linking in to its rail network. Yet Russia views with suspicion all projects which are perceived as reducing its earlier monopoly on Central Asian transport systems.

Bilateral cooperation

The political break-up of the Soviet Union was detrimental to economic relations between the former Soviet republics. The decision by the Russian government to focus on its domestic economic problems in 1992–3 resulted in a further reorientation of the economies of the new states away from Russia. The raising of the price of energy during the second part of 1993 had enormous repercussions, increasing the debts to Russia of the other CIS countries.[7]

Russia's trade with CIS countries has decreased drastically during the 1990s. This is in part a consequence of the blow to trade and economic relations following the break-up of the Soviet Union and a general decline in production and consumption, and in part due to a reorientation of trade in favour of Western countries. In 1990 trade with other Soviet republics constituted 69 per cent of Russia's total trade; by 1995 trade with other CIS countries made up only 18 per cent.[8] There is a difference in importance between exports and imports. The share of CIS countries in Russian imports is somewhat recovering, while their share in its exports is

[4] Ibid.
[5] Ibid.
[6] Peter Sinnott. 'Central Asia's Geographic Moment', *Central Asian Monitor*, no. 4, 1997.
[7] This may also be said of the price rise within the CIS from 20 per cent of European prices before May 1993 to 50–60 per cent during the second half of 1993. Akira Miyamoto, *Natural Gas in Central Asia: Industries, Markets and Export Options of Kazakstan, Turkmenistan and Uzbekistan*. London, RIIA, 1997, p. 8.
[8] S Razov, 'V novoi Tsentralnoi Azii', *Mezhdunarodnaya zhizn*, 1997, no. 3.

Table 1: Central Asia's share of Russia's total exports (%)

	1994	1995	1996	1997
Kazakhstan	2.6	3.4	3.1	1.7
Kyrgyzstan	0.2	0.1	0.2	0.2
Tajikistan	0.2	0.2	0.2	0.1
Turkmenistan	0.2	0.1	0.1	0.3
Uzbekistan	1.3	1.1	1.3	1.0

Sources: Calculated from data in International Monetary Fund, *Direction of Trade Statistics, Yearbook 1997,* Washington, DC, and *Quarterly Report*, June 1998.

Table 2: Central Asia's share of Russia's total imports (%)

	1994	1995	1996	1997
Kazakhstan	5.2	5.9	7.0	5.3
Kyrgyzstan	0.3	0.2	0.3	0.3
Tajikistan	0.2	0.4	0.2	0.2
Turkmenistan	0.2	0.2	0.3	0.3
Uzbekistan	2.2	1.9	1.5	1.9

Sources: Calculated from data in International Monetary Fund, *Direction of Trade Statistics, Yearbook 1997,* Washington, DC, and *Quarterly Report*, June 1998.

decreasing. Russian commentators are watching with concern the continuing process of decline in Russia's economic influence in trade and transport.[9] In December 1997 the Russian Ministry of Economics forecast that the CIS countries' share of Russia's total trade would continue to fall into the next century.[10]

Russia's commodity turnover with Central Asia in 1996 constituted only a third of its 1990 trade with the Soviet Central Asian republics. As shown in Tables 1 and 2, in 1997 Central Asian states made up only 3.3 per cent of Russia's total exports, and 8 per cent of its total imports. It must be stressed that statistics are not completely reliable since not all trade is recorded, notably the part which is undertaken by individual traders (known as 'shuttle traders') or through barter.

Another indicator of the trend of Russia's declining influence is the absence of new Russian investments in Central Asia outside the energy sector. There is virtually no Russian private capital in Uzbekistan, Turkmenistan, Kyrgyzstan and Tajikistan as the Central Asian markets open up and foreign capital flows into these

[9] *Kommersant-daily*, 28 May 1996; *Inside Central Asia*, no. 127, 24–30 June 1996, p. 6.
[10] Oleg Rybakov, 'Budushchii god – vremya proryva v sodruzheste', *Nezavisimaya gazeta*, 23 December 1997, p. 3.

countries. Several factors explain this situation. There is an underlying lack of financial resources for investments, but also an orientation towards intermediary operations of a financial-speculative character rather than investments. These structural weaknesses can be neither easily overcome nor compensated by the Russian state. Strict Russian regulations for capital export also contribute to the low level of Russian investments.

Russian experts have argued in favour of government support for investment in Central Asia. They warn that if the trend is allowed to continue, Russia runs the risk of being squeezed out of the Central Asian markets in the future. According to one Russian expert, 'it is evident that with regard to capital export and investment in Central Asia neither Russia nor other CIS states are able to compete with the rest of the world'.[11]

Kazakhstan

There are differences between the countries with regard to trade with Russia. Kazakhstan constitutes Russia's largest Central Asian trading partner, and Russia remains Kazakhstan's largest trading partner. Kazakhstan's trade with CIS countries fell drastically immediately after the break-up of the Soviet Union. The largest export and import commodity is fuel and oil products, which in 1996 constituted 33 per cent of Kazakhstan's total exports and 19 per cent of total imports.[12]

Russia's share of Kazakhstan's trade has fluctuated over the years (see Table 3).[13] Since 1995 there has been a continuous decline with regard to exports as well as imports. The statistics from the International Monetary Fund (*Direction of Trade Statistics*), which show recorded trade, indicate a trend of decline. How much unrecorded trade exists is impossible to say.[14]

Russia and Kazakhstan have blamed the charges and regulations imposed by national tariffs for the decline in trade. The Russian minister for cooperation with CIS States, Aman Tuleev, in a letter to the Kazakh first deputy Prime minister in January 1997, accused Kazakhstan of charging import duties on Russian goods 150 times above the rate previously agreed between the two countries.[15] The Customs Union has so far not been able to overcome these problems.

---

[11] A. Elyanov, 'Tsentralnaya Aziya, Perestroika mirokhozyaistvennykh otnoshenii', *Aziyai Afrika segodnya*, 1997, no. 11. p. 32.

[12] Economist Intelligence Unit, *Kazakhstan Country Profile, 1997–8*, p. 30.

[13] A. Elyanov, 'Tsentralnaya Aziya', p. 33. gives the figure of 57.3 per cent for Russia's share of Kazakhstan's total exports in 1991.

[14] Compare TACIS statistics: trade with Russia constituted 55 per cent of Kazakhstan's total imports in 1996 and 46 per cent in 1997. Russia's share of Kazakhstan's exports was 44.5 per cent in 1996 and 33.9 per cent in 1997. This lower level was maintained during the first quarter of 1998. TACIS statistics start from 1996.

[15] Itar-Tass, 29 January 1997; *Inside Central Asia*, no. 157, 27 January–2 February 1997.

Table 3: Russia's share of Kazakhstan's total exports and imports (%)

	1994	1995	1996	1997
Exports	63.1	61.1	44.5	38.1
Imports	49.3	62.1	55.0	47.9

Sources: Calculated from data in International Monetary Fund, *Direction of Trade Statistics, Yearbook 1997,* Washington, DC, and *Quarterly Report,* June 1998.

The seriousness of the challenge to Russia presented by Kazakhstan's economic diversification process is reflected in statistics on investment in Kazakhstan. Russia is only one of several investors and not among the largest. As already mentioned, by mid-1997 Kazakhstan had the fifth largest cumulative foreign direct investment value among all post-communist countries, ranking second only to Hungary in per-capita terms. More than 80 per cent of the most important enterprises in Kazakhstan were led by companies from the 'far abroad'. Foreign capital is finding its way to the sectors of metallurgy (50 per cent of foreign investments) and oil and gas (35 per cent).[16] According to Kazakhstan's State Committee on Statistics, by October 1996 there were 95 Russian joint ventures in Kazakhstan out of a total of 883 registered joint ventures. Tuleev accused Kazakhstan of acting to harm Russian economic interests, of deliberately avoiding the establishment of joint ventures and financial groups with Russia, and of selling off its natural resources to other countries. 'I have no moral right to keep silent about the fact that about 90 per cent of Kazakhstan's industry has been handed over to many third countries other than Russia,' he declared.

Uzbekistan

Uzbekistan's trade with the CIS as a whole and with Russia has been undergoing a radical decline. Russia remains the largest trade partner but its share of Uzbekistan's trade has been substantially reduced (see Table 4). According to the Russian expert Elyanov, Russia's share of Uzbekistan's total foreign trade turnover decreased from 53.9 per cent in 1990 to 14.4 per cent in 1996. Data on Uzbekistan's foreign trade are patchy and politically sensitive and estimates vary widely.[17] Yet the overall trend of a decrease in Uzbekistan's trade with Russia is clear.

[16] Kazakhstan CCG, Ch. 10 appendices. *BISNIS* home page. February 1998. According to TACIS estimates, Russia's share of Uzbekistan's total trade fell from 2.9 per cent in 1994 to 18.8 per cent in 1995. Its share of imports fell from 29.8 per cent (1994) to 24.9 per cent (1995).

[17] Economist Intelligence Unit, *Uzbekistan: Country Profile 1997–8,* p. 29; *Economic Trends, Quarterly Issue, Uzbekistan,* January–March 1998.

Table 4: Russia's share of Uzbekistan's total exports and imports (%)

	1994	1995	1996	1997
Exports	42.0	32.9	22.3	30.9
Imports	46.8	32.6	24.9	16.9

Sources: Calculated from data in International Monetary Fund, *Direction of Trade Statistics, Yearbook 1997,* Washington, DC, and *Quarterly Report*, June 1998.

The decline in trade between Uzbekistan and Russia is reflected in the falling level of cotton exports to Russia. Cotton is, together with gold, one of Uzbekistan's main exports and Russia has been the main recipient. In 1996 Uzbekistan lost the VAT-free protection for its cotton in Russia, as it did not become a member of the Customs Union.[18] As the Russian factories did not pay in hard currency, exports were cut. The dispute with regard to the cotton trade has not yet been resolved. Oil from Russia had previously constituted a large part of Uzbekistan's imports, but government policy in 1995 made the latter largely self-sufficient in energy. Machinery and foodstuffs now make up the largest import commodities.

A bilateral agreement was signed in March 1997 with the purpose of increasing trade, but so far it has had no results. Uzbekistan, declaring its interest in exporting to Russia, nevertheless decided to maintain export tariffs on important items such as gold, ferrous, non-ferrous and precious metals, oil, gas and cotton.[19]

Russia has an insignificant role to play in the increasing foreign investments in Uzbekistan.[20] According to estimates by the European Bank for Reconstruction and Development, annual foreign direct investment in Uzbekistan grew from $US85 million in 1994, to $US120 million in 1995 and $US150 million in 1996. With respect to the number of joint ventures, Turkey and the United States are the largest stakeholders, while South Korea, Indonesia, the UK, Germany and Japan are also major contributors in terms of investment volume.[21]

The increased degree of foreign investments reflects an increasing pragmatism by the Central Asian governments over who is investing in their countries. Such pragmatism was expressed by Uzbek President Karimov when he declared that 'Uzbekistan is open for everyone, and there is and there will be no ideology involved in the implementation of joint projects ... If it is beneficial for us, we will enhance relations even with the devil himself.'[22]

[18] Economist Intelligence Unit, *Uzbekistan: Country Profile 1997–8*, p. 32.
[19] Mekhman Gafarli, 'Rossiyu vytesnyayut s uzbekskogo rynka', *Nezavisimaya gazeta*, 23 December 1997, p. 3.
[20] Ibid.
[21] 'Uzbekistan: Trade and Investment Overview', *BISNIS* home page, February 1998.
[22] *Inside Central Asia*, no. 186, 18–24 August 1997, p. 3.

Table 5: Russia's share of Turkmenistan's total exports and imports (%)

	1994	1995	1996	1997
Exports	8.2	3.6	2.0	5.3
Imports	15.9	7.0	11.8	22.9

Sources: Calculated from data in International Monetary Fund, *Direction of Trade Statistics, Yearbook 1997,* Washington, DC, and *Quarterly Report*, June 1998.

Turkmenistan

Turkmenistan's trade with the CIS remains relatively substantial, but trade with Russia fell dramatically immediately after the break-up of the Soviet Union, and now constitutes only a small proportion of the total (see Table 5).[23] The export markets within the CIS are mainly Ukraine, Georgia, Armenia and Azerbaijan. Turkmenistan's exports to a very large extent consist of gas: in 1995 it made up 55.4 per cent of total exports, with cotton, the second item, constituting only 23 per cent.[24] In 1995, 67 per cent of total Turkmen exports went to CIS countries but only some 6 per cent to Russia. Again these figures vary somewhat according to different estimates. A notable characteristic of Turkmenistan's trade is its volatility and fluctuations caused by interruptions in gas trade as a result of disagreements with importer states over payment.

Tajikistan

In spite of the fact that Russia became militarily deeply involved in the Tajik civil war, its economic relations with Tajikistan have declined, and are today very limited. According to Elyanov, Russia's share of Tajikistan's total trade turnover decreased from 50.9 per cent in 1990 to 10.3 per cent in 1996.[25]

In 1995 Tajikistan's imports from Russia constituted only 6.7 per cent of its total imports, and exports to Russia only 8 per cent of total exports.[26] Aluminium was the principal export, when the Turzunzade plant was in operation, with Russia and Turkmenistan the largest importers of this commodity. In spite of this, other CIS states made up for the bulk of the CIS share of total imports (67.1 per cent), and of total exports (70.9 per cent). The major trading partners were Uzbekistan and Ukraine.[27]

---

[23] Elyanov, in 'Tsentralnaya Aziya', calculates that Russia's share of Turkmenistan's trade turnover fell from 47.5 per cent in 1990 to 6.6 per cent in 1996.

[24] Economist Intelligence Unit, *Kyrgyzstan, Tajikistan, Turkmenistan: Country Profile 1997–8*, p. 82.

[25] Elyanov, 'Tsentralnaya Aziya'.

[26] Economist Intelligence Unit, *Kyrgyzstan, Tajikistan, Turkmenistan: Country Profile 1997–8*. pp. 40–41.

[27] Economist Intelligence Unit, *Kyrgyzstan, Tajikistan, Turkmenistan: Country Report*, fourth quarter 1997, p. 55.

Russia's weak economic position *vis-à-vis* Tajikistan is reflected in the fact that today it is not among the major foreign investors there. Most joint ventures are within the sectors of natural resources, the two largest being with British mining companies.[28]

Kyrgyzstan

In Kyrgyzstan's trade there was a noticeable shift between 1991 and 1995 away from former Soviet countries. In 1990, 43.1 per cent of Kyrgyzstan's total trade had been with Russia, and about 50 per cent with the other Soviet republics together. In 1995 Russia's share of Kyrgyzstan's total exports was down to 25.6 per cent, and of imports 21.9 per cent.[29] The declining Russian economic influence is reflected in Kyrgyzstan's growing trade with China, which, as already mentioned, was its largest trading partner in 1997.

CIS economic cooperation

In September 1993 the member nations of the CIS agreed on the creation of an Economic Union to be established in a step-by-step process on the model of the European Union. The steps would include the development of a free trade zone, followed by a customs union and finally a payments and currency union to form a full economic union.[30] However, the decision has remained a declaration of intent, as the task of integrating economies undergoing a process of spontaneous disintegration, and at different levels of development and reform, was enormous.

In January 1995 Kazakhstan entered into a Customs Union with Russia and Belarus, which Kyrgyzstan subsequently joined. As a consequence of the failure to stimulate general CIS integration, in March 1996 these four states announced their decision to develop further economic integration by setting up a Quadrilateral Economic Union. The reform-oriented Russian press was sceptical of the new organization, suspecting the motives for its establishment to be political rather than economic. Nazarbayev, again demonstrating his willingness to enter multilateral cooperation, had not given up his concerns and views on the form and character of cooperative relations. In his comments about the Russian–Belarusian union created a few days earlier, he made it clear that Kazakhstan ruled out any development reminiscent of a revival of the USSR.[31] Later he warned against efforts to force integration on the CIS.[32]

---

[28] 'Tajikistan: Investment and Trade Overview', *BISNIS* home page, January 1998.
[29] Economist Intelligence Unit, *Kyrgyzstan, Tajikistan, Turkmenistan: Country Profile 1997–8*. p. 17.
[30] Mark Webber, *CIS Integration Trends: Russia and the Former Soviet South,* London, RIIA, 1997.
[31] *Inside Central Asia*, no. 113, 18–24 March 1996, p. 4.
[32] After the CIS Summit in March 1997, he declared that disintegration of the CIS would follow if integration were forced on the member states. *Inside Central Asia*, no. 165, 24–30 March 1997, p. 4.

With the creation of the Quadrilateral Economic Union Russia had intended to prove the success and benefits of integration on a small scale. Integration was not the outcome, however. The problems of creating a customs union were reflected by the continuing barriers to trade between the four member states inherent in their differing trade regulations, import tariffs, and kinds of quota on imported goods. The most important issues on the agenda at the meeting in October 1997 remained the harmonization of the profoundly different trading structures in operation and a reduction of the high tariffs on goods.

With the smaller summit of the Quadrilateral Economic Union preceding the CIS Summit in Kishinev in October 1997, Moscow intended to 'break the deadlock' over integration.[33] The Russian Deputy Prime Minister Valerii Serov admitted that 'the main question is how to breathe life into the quadripartite agreements of the Customs Union'. However, the meeting merely reflected the seriousness of the situation and the deep grievances of the non-Russian member states. Just before the meeting Kazakhstan's President Nazarbayev had, during a visit by Chernomyrdin to Almaty, for the first time publicly declared the unfeasibility of the present Customs Union.[34] At meetings with Leonid Kuchma, Nazarbayev and Akaev had criticized the existing tariffs and other trade barriers, laying the blame on Russia. Both Nazarbayev and Akaev claimed that Moscow's use of the Customs Union as a means for restricting trade was incompatible with normal relations and undermined the Customs Union.[35]

As a result, trade within the Customs Union continued to decline; it fell by 30 per cent in the first half of 1997, compared with the same period the previous year. The drop was attributed to the differing national legislations and the failure of member countries to coordinate their respective trade relationships with non-members.[36] The CIS member states found trade with other countries to be more advantageous, and cultivated trading partners further afield. Serov, worried by the centrifugal tendencies in the CIS, complained in November 1997 of certain CIS countries' 'unilateral actions in taking major economic decisions'.[37]

---

[33] As declared by Yeltsin's spokesman, Sergei Yastrzhembsky.
[34] Kozlov in *Nezavisimaya gazeta,* 7 October 1997, p. 3.
[35] Nazarbayev offered to export substantial amounts of oil to Ukraine and via Ukraine to Central Europe, but claimed that Russian tariff and transport practices stood in the way of such plans. Jamestown Foundation, *Monitor*, vol. 3, no. 197, 22 October 1997.
[36] According to Itar-Tass. *Jamestown Monitor*, no. 197, 22 October 1997.
[37] Interview in *Izvestiya,* 21 November 1997.

Cooperation between Russian and Central Asian regions

The enterprises in northern Kazakhstan are closely knit into a network of relations with their Russian counterparts, and are therefore vulnerable to problems in Russia. This is especially true with regard to energy industries which share a common infrastructure of pipelines and power networks. Russia provides electricity to its own Omsk region via grid lines across Kazakhstan.[38] Kazakhstan in turn imports electricity from Russia and has adversely been affected when electricity deliveries have been suspended. This has happened repeatedly owing to Kazakhstan's inability to honour its debts or to deliver coal in exchange.

The break-up of the Soviet Union was a heavy blow to the close relations between regions in Russia and Kazakhstan. While a few Russian financial-industrial groups extended into Kazakhstan,[39] the regions themselves had to be reorganized into the new state units of Russia and Kazakhstan. A deterioration in relations followed. This forced local leaders to act. Cross-border cooperation developed, and local leaders became key figures in external relations.

In an attempt to improve relations, Russian and Kazakhstani leaders sought to organize a regularized system of transborder contacts and meetings at regional level. In early 1995 an extensive bilateral treaty was signed which included provisions for increased contacts between regions in the two countries.[40] As a result an agreement on border cooperation was signed in Omsk between eleven Russian and nine Kazakhstani regions. A new phenomenon has thus appeared, whereby border regions have become lobby groups on important issues of external policy.[41]

Local leaders also saw the opportunities that had developed as a result of cross-border cooperation. In a situation where the central government was weak, local governments and industrial directors felt free to act, thereby strengthening their political position and improving the economic situation in the region. Russia's Altai Territory is one example of a region with a wish to rebuild relations with Kazakhstan. In August 1996 directors from major enterprises there visited their southern neighbours in Kazakhstan to renew economic ties that had slackened after the collapse of the USSR.[42] Tatarstan's leader Shamiyev visited Kazakhstan in August

[38] The Kazakh power and coal minister proposed the creation of a Russian–Kazakh joint stock company aimed at ensuring the transit of electricity supplies from Siberia to the Urals along Kazakhstan's power transmission lines. *Inside Central Asia*, no. 134, 12–18 August 1996, p. 4.
[39] Michael Kaser, *The Economies of Kazakstan and Uzbekistan*, London, RIIA, 1997, pp. 49–50.
[40] Neil Melvin, 'Southern Siberia and North-east Kazakhstan'.
[41] Ibid.
[42] As reported on Kazakh TV on 6 August 1996. Seven Altai company directors met the Kazakh trade and industry minister to discuss the creation of joint ventures between industries in Altai and in Kazakhstan. Particular interest was expressed in the Pavlodar tractor plant in the northeast of Kazakhstan, as Altai has for many years supplied Kazakhstan with engines and spare parts. *Inside Central Asia*, no. 133, 5–11 August 1996, p. 4.

1997 and discussed the expansion of bilateral trade, as the current trade turnover was considered inadequate. He also suggested cooperation in the oil industry.[43]

Other distant Russians regions have demonstrated their interest in developing direct economic relations. The mayor of Moscow, Luzhkov, visited Kazakhstan in August 1997 and signed several contracts: on the exchange of technology, the development of stock and security markets, trade and the economy, culture, education and tourism. He also signed an agreement on an annual supply of Kazakh grain to Moscow. Of greatest import was Luzhkov's interest in the purchase of two million tonnes of oil from Kazakh oilfields for Moscow's refineries, and possible Russian participation in developing Kazakhstan's oil- and gasfields at Tengiz, Karachaganak and on the Caspian shelf. Luzhkov and Nazarbayev also found common ground in their criticism of the CIS.[44]

Russian regional capital is now invested in Kazakh industry. A few examples may be mentioned. A Russian regional power grid was among the foreign investors which bought four opencast mines in Kazakhstan's giant Ekibastuz coalfield. Russia's Sverdlovskenergo company won ownership of the Kazakh Severnyy and part of the Bogatyr opencast mines. Sverdlovskenergo is a subsidiary of the Russian national grid monopoly Unified Energy System. The purchase safeguards regular supplies of cheap coal for power stations in the southern Urals and Omsk areas.[45]

Thus, while at a national level a process of reduced interdependence is taking place between Russia and the Central Asian states, at a local level economic relations are tending to grow. However, the process here is limited mainly to regions in Russia and Kazakhstan. In the other Central Asian states the predominant trend is one of a reduced Russian share of these countries' trade as a result of diversification.

It seems probable that the new Russian economic and financial crisis that erupted in August 1998 will increase the trend of diversification. The Central Asian leaders initially played down the effects on their own economies of the Russian crisis. Nazarbayev declared that the two countries' financial systems 'divorced long ago', and that the Russian rouble accounted only for about 7 per cent of commercial transactions in Kazakhstan. However, if the Russian crisis continues, the effects on the Central Asian economies may be much more significant. Therefore, as part of defending their economies, the Central Asian states can be expected to intensify their efforts to reorient their external economic relations away from Russia.

[43] *SWB* SU/3008 G/1, 27 August 1997. See also *Inside Central Asia*, no. 187, 25–31 August 1997.
[44] Luzhkov also said that the CIS was a 'nostalgic sham' and voiced support for Nazarbayev's Eurasian Union proposal: 'We need to return to the issue of forming a Eurasian Union, with full statehood, with full sovereignty [for each state], so that it should not scare anyone, but with a single economic space'. *SWB* SU/3005 G/3, 23 August 1997.
[45] *Inside Central Asia*, no. 144, 21–27 October 1996, p. 4. A Russian–Kazakh regional alliance has been created between Metallurgy Magnitogorsk and Rudnyi, *Nezavisimaya gazeta*, 12 September 1997, p. 3.

7 ENERGY

The independence of the Central Asian republics brought their assets of gas and oil in the Caspian basin to the forefront of international attention. The new states, aware that their energy resources could help them towards economic growth and wealth and eager to initiate economic development, began to seek investors and financial assistance. Discussions with potential foreign partners began as early as 1991–2. Finding an outlet for the export of oil and gas to foreign markets beyond the CIS soon appeared as the key issue.

The Central Asian states need to resolve the problem of outlets if they are ever to be independent in a more than formal sense. To Russia, the manner in which this is done is a crucial issue, since continued control of energy transportation would allow it to maintain its influence in Central Asia, and it is therefore concerned at the growing international interest in the exploitation of the region's gas and oil. To Russia, such attention is as novel as it is for the Central Asian states, yet for a long time it failed to adapt to the change. Policy-makers in Russia reacted differently to the situation. The government saw it mainly as an issue of how to maintain influence and prevent foreign penetration of Central Asia and the Caspian region. To Russian companies it became of paramount importance both to participate in order to gain economically from the new situation while blocking foreign companies from access, and to prevent the Central Asians themselves from becoming competitors in energy exports. With such different priorities, the Russians did not always behave in a consistent and coherent way.

The race for energy had made Central Asia into a field for a new 'great game' but in the context of the twenty-first century. Shares, influence and control over the natural resources of oil and gas are at issue. In this game the national interests of the Central Asian states now make them look beyond Russia.

An energy system controlled by Russia

With regard to oil, gas and electricity the Central Asian states are interlinked in a complex network of pipelines and electricity grids processing facilities and supply. All the states, to a greater or lesser extent, depend upon one another but also upon cooperation with Russia. Russia has been and still is at the centre of the energy web from which Kazakhstan, Turkmenistan and Uzbekistan are now trying to disengage.[1]

The shared network of electricity grids offers a good example.[2] The Central Asian countries are linked to a grid which assumes a high net level of imports from neighbouring countries. The exchanges between them are based on an annual balance of supply of electrical energy imports and exports. Kazakhstan, the only country bordering on Russia, is directly linked to Russia by a northern system, and to the Central Asian countries by a southern one, but with no link between these two systems.

Kazakhstan has huge reserves of oil and natural gas, the largest oilfields being Tengiz, Karachaganak, Uzen and Kumkola to the northwest of the Caspian Sea. Kazakhstan also has significant resources in the Caspian Sea. Yet energy products remain one of its main imports, comprising, in 1995, 26 per cent of total imports.[3] This has been due to a lack of infrastructure, such as oil and gas processing facilities, pipelines and power stations.[4] Although Kazakhstan's resources of oil and gas are mainly located in the west of the country most of the industrial capacity is located in the major cities in the east and southeast of the country. The crude oil produced in the west is pumped north to refineries in southern Russia and from there supplied to the rest of the former Soviet Union.[5] The oil required in the east of the country is obtained from crude pumped south from western Siberia and refined at Pavlodar (Russia) or Chimkent (Uzbekistan). There has been no pipeline connecting the east and the west of the country. The internal gas transportation system has been poorly developed; it is limited to the western and southern parts of Kazakhstan, and is for domestic consumption alone.[6] For consumption in other parts of the country, gas is imported from Turkmenistan, Uzbekistan and Russia. The government of Kazakhstan has given high priority to the development of the gas pipeline grid.

Uzbekistan was dependent on energy imports until 1995, when it became self-sufficient. In 1990 it imported around three-quarters of its oil requirements from Russia and Kazakhstan. Uzbekistan has oil and gas deposits in the Amu Darya Basin in the southwest of the country (near Bukhara), in the east in the Fergana Depression, and in the south of the Aral Sea, but these reserves cannot be compared with those of Kazakhstan or Turkmenistan. As a result of its deliberate decision to

---

[1] Gavan McDonell, *The Euro-Asian Corridor*, pp. 15–21 (see above, Chapter 6, note 3).

[2] Ibid., p. 21.

[3] Oil products accounted for 12.0 per cent and natural gas comprised 9.7 per cent. See Miyamoto, *Natural Gas in Central Asia* (see above, Chapter 6, note 7).

[4] Ibid., p. 21.

[5] McDonell, *The Euro-Asian Corridor*, p. 15.

[6] Yuzhno-Kazakhstan, Zhambyl and Almaty oblasts in southern Kazakhstan, and Kustani and Mangistau in the west are the major consuming areas. See Miyamoto, *Natural Gas in Central Asia*.

meet domestic needs following the collapse of the Soviet Union, when the energy trade among CIS countries suffered disruption, Uzbekistan concentrated on increasing its own energy production so as to strengthen its independence. The policy of achieving self-sufficiency in energy, with regard to both production and refining capacities, was viewed as one of the chief means of reducing Russia's influence.[7] Uzbek policy has been successful in this and the country is exporting gas to neighbouring Tajikistan, Kyrgyzstan and Kazakhstan via existing pipeline systems.

Turkmenistan is heavily dependent on its neighbours on energy issues, but in a different way. It developed a more trade-dependent economy than most other republics in the former Soviet Union, and was the second largest gas supplier after Russia. It earned hard currency from exports to Europe through an exchange arrangement with the Russian republic which sent gas to Europe in return for the supply of Turkmen gas to other parts of the Soviet Union. In 1993 natural gas accounted for 74 per cent of total exports.[8] Turkmenistan has large oil reserves, but its natural gas reserves are vast – the world's fourth largest.[9] Since 1992 Turkmen gas exports to CIS countries have been curtailed or temporarily interrupted owing to reduced demand on the CIS markets but also to the CIS countries' inability to pay. The main importers of Turkmen gas are Ukraine, Georgia and Armenia. Turkmenistan has also had disputes with Russia concerning gas export arrangements and the increased tariffs on gas transport.

A crucial aspect of the common energy legacy is that the pipeline system that would provide an outlet to foreign markets for Central Asian countries runs across Russian territory and is controlled by Russian companies. This means that if the Central Asians are to capitalize on their vast oil and gas reserves, they need Russian cooperation and access to Russia's pipelines and port facilities. The existing pipeline system for gas is now owned and administered by the Russian gas monopoly Gazprom. There are four access points for pipelines from Kazakhstan into Russia. Turkmen gas links up with pipelines in Kazakhstan at Beyneu. The pipeline system for oil is run by the Russian companies Transneft and Lukoil. One line connects Tengiz and Karachaganak in Kazakhstan with Samara in Russia. Another runs via Tikhoretsk to the Russian Black Sea port of Novorossiisk.

However, these outlets for Kazakhstan and Turkmenistan exist mainly in theory. Some parts of the pipelines have been taken out of service and need repairing and extending before they can be used again, particularly if oil and gas production increases.

[7] Miyamoto, *Natural Gas in Central Asia*, pp. 54–5; McDonell, *The Euro-Asian Corridor*, p. 19.
[8] Miyamoto, *Natural Gas in Central Asia*, p. 49.
[9] Ottar Skagen, *Caspian Gas*, London, RIIA, 1997, p. 8.

Existing outlets

Russia faces a dilemma in its policy towards Central Asia and the Caspian region. The overriding interest within the government is to maintain control and obstruct all attempts at shifting influence to out-of-region states. Conflicting interests are also developing within Russian business, which on the one hand is making it difficult for Central Asia to compete abroad and on the other wants to participate in the new race for Central Asian energy exploitation. These conflicting interests are reflected in Russia's not always consistent foreign policy manoeuvring. Since the main pipeline systems run across its territory, Russia is able to control how much gas or oil – if any – the Central Asian states are allowed to transport. The possibility of limiting or cutting off supplies gives it a unique political or commercial lever.

In an interview in May 1997 Nazarbayev warned that 'a great desire to squeeze us and bring us to our knees has emerged from Russia's industrialists and state ministries'. Russia's efforts to control gas exports from Central Asia to prevent competition with its own gas exports is clearly reflected in the case of gas from Kazakhstan's main gas field at Karachaganak. The field is located not far from the Russian border and only a few hundred kilometres from the Russian town of Orenburg, the starting point for the Soyuz pipeline used for exports to Europe.[10] It would be easy to have Kazakh gas linked up to the Soyuz line. However, Rem Vyakhirev, director of the Russian gas monopoly Gazprom, declared at a news conference in August 1997 that his company 'would under no circumstances' agree to give Kazakh gas an outlet through Russia to world markets: 'Surrendering one's market when there is a lack of sufficient capacity is, I believe, nothing less than a crime against Russia.' He also declared that only a certain amount of Kazakh gas could be accepted for processing in Orenburg.[11]

Kazakh oil from the Tengiz field is being transported through Russian pipelines for export to non-CIS markets, but only a restricted volume. As a consequence, oil production at Tengiz has been held back during the past few years. The reason given for the restriction is the competing need to use the pipelines for Russia's own oil exports.

The reasons for Russia's obstruction of Turkmen gas exports can also to a large extent be viewed as commercial. With a strong interest in expanding further into European markets in general and into Turkey in particular, Russia does not allow Turkmen gas to compete in these markets. In November 1996, during a visit to Turkmenistan by Vyakhirev, an agreement was reached on the export of Turkmen natural gas to western Europe, but Russia did not comply with its terms.[12] In August

[10] Miyamoto, *Natural Gas in Central Asia*, p. xvii.
[11] *Inside Central Asia*, no. 184, 4–10 August 1997, p. 4.
[12] Itar-Tass, 9 November 1996. Reported by *Inside Central Asia*, no. 146, 4–10 November 1996, p. 3.

1997, after a meeting with Chernomyrdin and Vyakhirev, President Niyazov accused Russia of hampering Turkmenistan's attempts to export its gas to European markets and attempting to confine its exports to the indebted customers of the CIS: 'Yesterday, in my conversation with Chernomyrdin and Vyakhirev, I had the feeling I was up against old Soviet ambitions, when they tried to say: "Very well, we will do without your gas." I also said, "Fine, you do without it, and we will do without you too".'[13]

Russia wants Turkmenistan to concentrate on CIS markets. However, the demand for energy on CIS markets in general was reduced following the fall in production, and when former customers of Turkmen gas were not able to pay for their supplies. As a consequence of unpaid debts, above all from Ukraine, Turkmenistan cut its gas exports. When Gazprom demanded increased prices and tariffs for the transport of gas to Ukraine, the margin of profit for Turkmenistan was reduced. In March 1997 Turkmen exports to Ukraine were completely cut off as a result of Turkmenistan's dispute with Gazprom over the pricing of transport.[14] Gazprom, with its vast supplies of gas, replaced Turkmen gas deliveries to Ukraine.

It is in the Russian government's interest to maintain control over Central Asian outlets. However, Gazprom's commercial interest in preventing Turkmenistan from competing with Russian gas exports by limiting access to the Russian pipelines may be against the Russian government's strategic interest of maintaining overall control. This was illustrated when Chernomyrdin promised in February 1998 that an agreement between Gazprom and Turkmenistan was close, but Gazprom pulled out. The more Gazprom obstructs, the more eager the Turkmen government will become to find alternative outlets for its gas. To the Russian government this causes a dilemma, since Turkmenistan arranged for a new temporary outlet through Iran which can be extended further. A similar situation is evolving with regard to Lukoil and Transneft in their attempts to restrict the export of oil from Kazakhstan. Apart from small-scale arrangements with Iran and Azerbaijan to exchange oil for export, Kazakhstan remains dependent on Russian outlets.

Exploitation and financing

Russia has put a lot of effort into becoming a partner in the international consortia that have been set up. Moscow made an aggressive bid for a stake in the lucrative oil deals, pushed hard for a share in Tengizchevroil, one of the former Soviet Union's largest joint ventures, and was successful in securing a 15 per cent share for

[13] *Inside Central Asia*, no. 184, 4–10 August 1997, pp. 1 and 6.
[14] Ashir Ioliev, 'Eksport turkmenskogo gaza: nevynuzhdennye eksperimenty prodolzhayutsya', *Tsentralnaya Aziya* (published in Sweden), no. 6 (12), 1997.

Gazprom in the Karachaganak field in Kazakhstan. In addition, it exercised leverage over companies in the Caspian region by putting pressure on their holdings in Russia.[15]

The Karachaganak field constitutes a large oil and gas condensate reservoir. In 1992 Kazakhstan signed an agreement with British Gas and Italian Agip to reactivate the field. In February 1995 Kazakhstan brought Gazprom into the deal after threats to block the export of Karachaganak's oil and gas, and to purchase the field's output at no more than 15 per cent of world prices unless Gazprom was included in the project.[16] In 1996, Gazprom sold its stake in the project to the Russian company Lukoil. Lukoil, however, has cash-flow problems and has no access to the gas pipelines controlled by Gazprom. Sponsors of the project have come to regard the export of Karachaganak gas to markets outside the CIS as a fairly distant prospect.[17]

The largest development project is the Tengiz field in northwestern Kazakhstan. Lukoil joined the consortium in January 1997 with a 5 per cent stake. As early as 1992 Kazakhstan had signed a contract with the American company Chevron to exploit the reserves of oil at the Tengiz field. However, as the question of an outlet for its oil had not been resolved, Lukoil was made a partner in 1996 to secure a Russian interest. The Caspian Pipeline Consortium (CPC) was set up in 1992 by Kazakhstan, Russia and Oman, in order to secure the transportation of oil from Tengiz to Novorossiisk for transport on to international markets. As the CPC did not develop as planned, Tengiz oil production was held back.

The Caspian Pipeline Consortium is thus a key project as it holds the future flow of Tengiz oil across Russia in its hands. The delay to the project, partly a result of Russia's lack of interest, which stemmed from the lack of necessary capital, became a central policy problem, and Nazarbayev personally pleaded to Chevron for Lukoil to be included in the project to secure a Russian interest in its success.[18] In April 1996 the problem seemed to have come closer to a solution when Kazakhstan, Oman and Russia, after months of deadlock over the allocation of shares, agreed to reduce their shares in the CPC from 100 per cent to 50 per cent (Russia 24 per cent, Kazakhstan 19 per cent and Oman 7 per cent). This made it possible for other international oil companies to invest in the project. In December 1996 a package of

[15] Rosemarie Forsythe, *The Politics of Oil in the Caucasus and Central Asia: Prospects for Oil Exploration and Export in the Caucasian Basin*, Adelphi Paper 300, Oxford, International Institute for Strategic Studies, 1996, p. 16.
[16] Ibid., p. 42.
[17] Ottar Skagen, *Caspian Gas,* p. 20.
[18] *Nezavisimaya gazeta* reported in January 1996 that the transport of Kazakh oil had become a foreign policy problem of high priority to the Kazakh president. Sergei Kozlov, 'Nazarbaevu nadoeli obeshchaniya', *Nezavisimaya gazeta*, 19 January 1996.

agreements was signed in Moscow between the governments of the three countries together with a group of international oil companies of the CPC, whereby the shares owned by the Russian state and by Russian companies constituted over 40 per cent of equity, and a Russian Lukoil representative was chosen to head the consortium.[19]

At that time both Nazarbayev and Yeltsin were satisfied with the deal:

> For two to three years we have been unable to solve the problem of constructing the pipeline ... At last we have settled it today and the consortium has been set up. The construction of the pipeline will start, and we would hope that the first phase will take a year and that in approximately two or two and half years it will all be finished. This will remove any insinuations and speculation about the transportation of Kazakh oil in any different direction. This issue is removed from the agenda for at least the next ten years.

Yeltsin, who had for a long time disagreed with the allocation of shares in the project, said: 'now we are satisfied with the stake we have received'.

However, Russia did not rush to implement the deal on the CPC. In an interview in September 1997, the Kazakh foreign minister Tokayev complained that he found the Russian position hard to understand. As soon as Russia had got the lion's share of the Caspian Sea consortium, he said, it was no longer in a hurry to develop it.[20] The delay in the construction of the pipeline from Tengiz to Novorossiisk contributed to the increasing tensions between the two countries.

A new, more aggressively competitive approach by the Russian government on energy issues and investment was reflected in Nemtsov's statements in November 1997, when he called for more active Russian involvement in developing the Caspian oilfields to counter growing Western influence in the region.[21] He argued that Russians must be 'leaders rather than outsiders' in the Caspian region and that Russia had already begun to play a 'more dynamic' role there. Describing the Caspian region as 'another Persian Gulf', Nemtsov said Russia had wasted valuable time and was lagging behind American and British investment companies in Azerbaijan: 'Unfortunately, we have been losing time up to now, and the Americans have shored up their positions. Suffice it to say that US companies – Amoco, Exxon, Mobil and others, as well as Britain's BP – are involved in practically every

---

[19] John Roberts, *Caspian Pipelines*, London, RIIA, 1996, pp. 31–2. In October 1997 the following companies participated: Chevron (US), LUKARKO (Russia–USA), Rosneft–Shell (Russia–the Netherlands), Mobil (USA), Agip (Italy), British Gas (UK), Kazakhstan Pipeline (Kazakhstan–USA), and Oryx (US). *Nezavisimaya gazeta*, 17 October 1997, p. 3.

[21] *Nezavisimaya gazeta*, 18 September 1997, p. 3.

[21] *Inside Central Asia*, no. 199, 17–23 November 1997, p. 6.

new oilfield being developed in Azerbaijan.' Nemtsov, however, was not against foreign investment in oil exploitation as long as Russia was to maintain a leading role.

Yet, despite having become a partner in the international consortia for the exploitation of the oil and gas resources of Central Asia, Russia has so far not shown any serious interest in realizing these projects.

Potential outlets

As a reaction to Russia's use of its monopoly of the pipeline system for oil and gas outlets, Kazakhstan and Turkmenistan started to seek alternative routes. Russia, in turn, has strongly reacted to such proposals, trying to maintain its overall control.

In the short term Kazakhstan and Turkmenistan have found temporary alternatives. Oil is shipped across the Caspian Sea to Baku, from where it is piped to Azerbaijani processing facilities for local use. An equivalent amount of Azerbaijani oil is then sent by rail across the Caucasus to Batumi. Another attempt has been to ship oil to an Iranian port on the Caspian coast for processing there, while an equivalent volume of crude oil is made available at a Persian Gulf port.[22] In January 1998 a first trainload of oil from Tengiz arrived in China.[23] Turkmenistan too has started to reorient its trade and energy export southwards. A 200-km pipeline linking its Korpedzhe gasfield to Kord-Kuy in northern Iran began operations in December 1997. The Kord-Kuy link is significant, as this connection to the Iranian network provides the first pipeline for further export.

Several long-term options remain open to discussion. It remains a moot question which, if any of these, will be realized. The question of financing has not been resolved as many factors of risk and insecurity are involved.

For Turkmen gas the main options are southward routes. The 200-km stretch of the pipeline to Kord-Kuy is part of a plan agreed in 1992 for extension to a 3,500-km pipeline carrying gas to consumers in Turkey and Europe. An alternative option from Kord-Kuy exists: a link to the Iranian pipeline system for transport down to the Persian Gulf.[24] A route via northern Iran into Turkey would be the shortest and is therefore attractive, but strong resistance from the US Congress towards Iran has so far stalled the project. Turkmenistan is eager to fulfil these plans. Another option is to build a pipeline across Afghanistan to Pakistan. In March

[22] Peter Sinnott, 'Central Asia's Geographic Moment' , *Central Asia Monitor*, 1997, no. 4, p. 24.
[23] Jamestown Foundation, *Monitor*, vol. 4, no. 11, 19 January 1998.
[24] In October 1997 Niyazov signed three protocols of intent with Iran, one of which concerned the construction of an oil pipeline from Turkmenistan's Caspian shore across Iran to the coast, the other two concerned the linking of the Korpedzhe–Kord-Kuy line to the Iranian grid and the construction of a transcontinental gas pipeline from Turkmenistan to Turkey via Iran. RFE/RL Newsline, no. 138, 14 October 1997; Jamestown Foundation, *Monitor*, vol. 3, no. 193, 16 October 1997.

1995 a consortium of UNOCAL, Delta and Gazprom agreed to set up a consortium to develop Turkmen gas reserves and build a pipeline to Pakistan.[25] War and the instability in Afghanistan following the Taliban takeover made such a route seem insecure. In February 1998 Gazprom pulled out of the project.

For Kazakh gas there seem to be no alternative outlets. With regard to oil, options exist in four directions. To the north there are options offered by the CPC to repair and extend connections with the Russian Black Sea port of Novorossisk.[26] The southern option would transport Tengiz oil via Baku in Azerbaijan to the Turkish Mediterranean port of Ceyhan. In September 1997, during the Turkish prime minister's visit to Almaty, Nazarbayev seemed to have given priority to this route.[27] However, an eastern option appeared when Kazakhstan, in the same month, signed a $9.5 billion agreement with the China National Petroleum Corporation (CNPC) to construct a 3,000-kilometre oil pipeline from Kazakhstan to China's northwestern Xinjiang region. The construction of the pipeline to China is supposed to be completed in five years' time.[28] If the Chinese pipeline connection were to be built it would open a possible option for Turkmenistan to link up to it as well. The agreement with China also included the construction of a 250-km pipeline from Kazakhstan to the Turkmen border for further extension to Iran. For Kazakhstan the option of routes crossing Iran's territory to export oil remains, despite US criticism. After Nazarbayev's visit to the United States, he announced that economic reasons alone would determine which pipelines would be built.[29]

So far no final decisions have been taken with regard to long-term pipeline options other than the CPC line across Russian territory. All projects demand large investments and these have not been resolved. As estimates of the energy resources of Central Asia have risen in recent years as a result of the more sophisticated technology and geophysical expertise brought into the region by Western companies, the interest of foreign investors and companies has intensified. Feasibility studies are being carried out and memoranda and agreements are being signed. All this suggests that the Central Asian states will become less dependent on the former Soviet energy grid.

[25] *Inside Central Asia*, no. 133, 5–11 August 1996, p. 5.
[26] See John Roberts, *Caspian Pipelines*.
[27] *Nezavisimaya gazeta*, 12 September 1997; *Inside Central Asia*, no. 189, 8–14 September 1997, p. 3.
[28] The two countries are to develop oil- and gasfields in Uzen, western Kazakhstan, and in the northern Aktyubinsk region. *Inside Central Asia*, no. 191, 22–28 September 1997, pp. 1 and 4.
[29] *Inside Central Asia*, no. 202, 8–14 December 1997, p. 4.

The legal status of the Caspian Sea

The legal status of the Caspian Sea is central to the question of who owns the right to exploit its energy resources and transport energy resources across or under it.

Russian policy with regard to the Caspian Sea crystallized in 1994. In 1993, when the five Caspian littoral states met to discuss common issues in connection with it, Kazakhstan presented a proposal to divide the sea into national sectors with equidistant boundaries from the shores of the bordering states. This was according to the UN Law of the Sea Convention of 1982. It was also a practice that had developed between the Soviet republics. Russia gave a sharp response to Kazakhstan's proposal and to Turkmenistan's declaration of a 12-mile zone of territorial water as well as an additional economic zone. In its document 'The Russian Federation on the question of the legal status of the Caspian Sea' of 6 October 1994, Russia claimed that the 1921 and 1940 treaties between the Soviet Union and Iran would apply until a change of status had jointly been decided upon by the five littoral states. These two treaties had implied the joint use of the Caspian Sea, closing it to all third parties. Furthermore, Russia claimed that the 1982 UN Convention could not apply since the Caspian Sea should be considered a 'lake'.[30] Under a division into the proposed national sectors few if any substantial resources would be in Russia's sector. On the other hand, if the Caspian were regarded as a lake, then its central area would be held in common and assets such as gas and oil divided evenly.

This intransigence was reflected in the then Foreign Minister Andrei Kozyrev's use of the unresolved Caspian demarcation as a means to oppose the first major Azeri international oil consortium agreement in 1994. In October of the same year, Russia declared in a paper circulating within the UN that Moscow reserved the right to take 'appropriate measures' against Caspian states that unilaterally began exploring the Caspian seabed.[31] However, departmental differences existed. In November 1993 the Russian Fuel and Energy Minister Yuri Shafranik signed an agreement with Azerbaijan that recognized an Azeri sector of the Caspian Sea.[32] Differences of this kind persisted, leading to a lack of policy coordination. In time Moscow came to alienate both Turkmenistan and Kazakhstan.

The issue of the division of the Caspian Sea developed into a serious territorial dispute between Russia and Kazakhstan. With no agreement on the northeastern part of the sea, Russia did not recognize Kazakh preparations for exploitation in an area which Kazakhstan considers its own.[33] Russia thus reacted angrily to the announcement

[30] L. Sklyarov, 'Kaspiiskii region: sotrudnichestvo ili sopernichestvo?', *Aziya i Afrika segodnya*, 1996, no. 9.
[31] Rosemarie Forsythe, *The Politics of Oil*, p. 30.
[32] Ibid., p. 29.
[33] *Nezavisimaya gazeta*, 7 October 1997.

of a Kazakh tender in the disputed corner of the Caspian Sea. Since Kazakhstan had, after independence, started to look for foreign investors to develop the Tengiz oilfields of Mangyshlak, it came under criticism from Russia, which claimed that Tengiz exploitation violated the USSR–Iran agreement on the Caspian Sea. The conflict developed as Russia itself announced a tender for oil exploitation in the northeast of the Caspian Sea.[34]

A conflict developed with Turkmenistan as well, despite the fact that it had at first seemed to share Russia's and Iran's stand on the issue. Russia, Turkmenistan and Iran had agreed in November 1996 to set up a company for the joint exploration and exploitation of oil and mineral resources in the Caspian Sea. They declared that Kazakhstan and Azerbaijan were welcome to join. Iran and Turkmenistan also supported a Russian proposal for the Caspian states to control a 72-km zone off their shores, with the rest of the sea to be jointly owned.[35] However, Turkmenistan's stance was not consistent. In October 1994, President Niyazov publicly supported Azerbaijan's right to develop its Caspian sector.[36] As pointed out by the adviser to the President of Azerbaijan, Gulizade, Turkmenistan had *de facto* recognized the division into national sectors when the Turkmen authorities started seeking the use of a Caspian network of pipelines.[37]

Relations with Turkmenistan reached crisis point as a consequence of Russia's handling of the territorial issue. In February 1997 Turkmenistan joined Kazakhstan in a statement demanding the temporary division of the sea into national sectors, pending a final decision on its legal status. Each state would prospect for and extract mineral resources in its own section.[38] The Russian Foreign Ministry ignored this event and denied media reports that the Kazakh–Turkmen statement left Moscow 'in almost total isolation', contending that it gave 'no ground for such interpretations', but it did acknowledge that the statement contained provisions which differed from the Russian stance on the issue, and as such would 'hardly ... be accepted'.[39] A spokesman for the Russian Foreign Ministry rejected the claim by Turkmenistan that some of the Caspian offshore oilfields should be jointly developed by Russia and Azerbaijan.[40]

Turkmenistan reacted strongly to the Russian–Azeri deal in July 1997 (Lukoil, Rosneft and Azerbaijan's SOCAR) to develop the disputed Kyapaz/Serdar oilfield

[34] Tokayev in *Nezavisimaya gazeta*, 18 September 1997, p. 3.
[35] *Inside Central Asia*, no. 150, 2–8 December 1996, p. 6.
[36] Rosemarie Forsythe, *The Politics of Oil*, p. 31.
[37] *Inside Central Asia*, no. 200, 24–30 November 1997, p. 5.
[38] *Inside Central Asia*, no. 161, 24 February–2 March 1997, p. 4.
[39] *Inside Central Asia*, no. 162, 3–9 March 1997, p. 6.
[40] Gennadii Tarasov said that 'the Caspian Sea is common property' and that Russia supported a 'temporary legal mechanism' in line with the 1921 and 1940 Soviet–Iranian treaties until the sea's status had been resolved. *Inside Central Asia*, no. 159, 10–16 February 1997, p. 3.

in the Caspian Sea. At first, Russia remained silent in the face of the Turkmen protest. As a crisis in relations developed towards the end of July, a Russian delegation under the Deputy Prime Minister Valerii Serov went to Turkmenistan to apologize and at the same time justify the earlier agreement with Azerbaijan.[41] By the time the meeting between the two presidents, Yeltsin and Niyazov, had been convened on 7 August 1997, Russia had bowed to the Turkmen criticism. The Russian government persuaded Lukoil/Rosneft to withdraw from the contract signed with SOCAR in early July to develop the disputed field. Yeltsin said the contract had been 'a mistake' and explained that it had been signed without consulting presidential or government authorities. The Russian presidential spokesman Yastrzhembsky not only further stressed that the contract had been signed 'behind the back of the Foreign Ministry', but also admitted that this practice was 'rather common' in Russia. He called upon Russian businessmen 'to show a spirit of cooperation with the Foreign Ministry' and added that 'it will pay off'. A joint communiqué between Yeltsin and Niyazov reiterated the need to adhere to the 1940 treaty between the USSR and Iran and the joint use of the sea until a new status had been settled.

Only one week after the presidents had met and the agreement had been cancelled, Turkmen TV announced an international tender to prospect for and extract oil and gas in the Turkmen sector of the Caspian Sea.[42]

Russia has not been successful in gaining support for its proposal for joint use of the Caspian Sea. The legal status of the sea has not yet been decided upon. The five-state meeting in May 1997 showed that negotiations remained deadlocked.[43] Russia, facing a *fait accompli* of eventual division of the Caspian Sea into national sectors, started to change its tack. In February 1998 it was reported that Russia had proposed a division of the seabed into national sectors, but not of the surface or of the water itself.[44] This indicated that Russia had abandoned its 1996 proposal for a 72-km zone of national jurisdiction. In April 1998 Russia and Kazakhstan signed an agreement dividing the seabed into national sectors.

The Russian change of policy opens up the possibilities for national exploitation within the respective zones, but leaves all issues of transportation to joint decisions between all littoral states. As such, the proposal also fits into the Russian government's strategic objective of maintaining influence over pipeline routes.

---

[41] *Nezavisimaya gazeta*, 30 July 1997.
[42] *Inside Central Asia*, no. 185, 11–17 August 1997, p. 6.
[43] Sergei Kozlov, 'Dlya neftyanykh kompanii status Kaspiya ne imeet znacheniya', *Nezavisimaya gazeta*, 19 August 1997, p. 3.
[44] 'Rossiya vyrabotala novye predlozheniya po statusu Kaspiya i namerena nachat ikh obsuzhdenie s Kazakhstana', Interfax, 9 February 1998; 'New Russian Initiative on Caspian Demarcation Announced', BBC Monitoring Service, 11 February 1998.

Conflicting Russian interests

In the energy sector Russia still maintains influence and control. However, as the commercial interests of Russian companies develop, they create a conflict of interests with the Russian government.

In the long term, Central Asian energy exports constitute a potential competitor to Russian energy exports. Gazprom and the large Russian oil companies are concentrating on expanding their foreign markets. Energy generates 40 per cent of Russia's total budget revenues and over half of its export revenues.[45] Russia is one of the largest gas exporters in the world. During the 1990s its gas production and export increased and today gas is a larger export commodity than oil. Gazprom's strategy has become one of expansion in the European market as well as in markets to the east and to the south. Gazprom's efforts to make a breakthrough in foreign markets are evident, and are affecting Russian policy with regard to the Central Asian states.

One target in the strategy to expand further into Europe is Turkey, which Turkmenistan also views as a future market for gas exports. In December 1997 Russia signed an agreement with Turkey on the export of gas and the construction of a pipeline. For Russia it was a project of great importance, since it meant access not only to the Turkish but also to southeast European and Middle Eastern markets. Russia's agreement with Turkey reflects Russia's determination to confirm its position as gas exporter to Turkey before Turkmenistan does. Against this background, Gazprom is hardly likely to allow Turkmenistan an outlet to the European market across Russia.

Another target is the Asian market, and in 1997 Russia's strategy became more pronounced.[46] In June 1997 the Russian Prime Minister Chernomyrdin visited Beijing and signed an agreement to export natural gas and electricity from east Siberia to China. In October 1997 Vyakhirev confirmed plans to export gas to China, and in November 1997, at the time of Yeltsin's visit to China, an intergovernmental framework agreement was signed on the building of a gas pipeline from the Siberian field of Kovytkinsk to Shanghai.[47] Kovytkinsk is one of two major fields in the Irkutsk region. Gazprom has several projects under discussion, thus further underlining the importance attributed to the Asian markets.[48]

Here Kazakhstan may one day become a competitor to Russia. In the very long term the demand for energy in the expanding Chinese and East Asian markets may be large enough to absorb exports from both countries, and even Turkmenistan. In

[45] Khripunov and Matthews, 'Russia's Oil and Gas Interest Group', p. 39 (see above, Chapter 3, note 18).
[46] Keun-Wook Paik and Jae-Yong Choi, *Pipeline Gas in Northeast Asia: Recent Developments and Regional Perspectives*, Briefing Paper no. 39, London, RIIA, January 1998.
[47] Dimitrii Kosyrev and Stanislav Petrov, 'Den grustnykh ulybok v Pekine', *Nezavisimaya gazeta*, 11 November 1997, pp. 1 and 2.
[48] Paik and Choi, *Pipeline Gas in Northeast Asia*.

the medium term the problem of finding investors and financial backers for such huge projects will turn Russia and Kazakhstan into competitors.

It seems evident that the Russian government has become much more aware of the power of energy issues as a lever for its foreign policy. From the perspective of Russian interests in controlling energy outlets, Moscow is anxiously observing all plans for an oil pipeline across the Caucasus and beyond Russian territory. Moscow read with concern the communiqué of March 1998, signed by the foreign ministers of Turkmenistan, Kazakhstan, Azerbaijan, Georgia and Turkey, announcing the construction of a pipeline from Baku to Ceyhan with links across the Caspian Sea.

The government and Gazprom have common strategic interests not to allow Central Asian gas to reach foreign markets except via the Russian pipeline system. However, Russian companies are to an increasing degree following commercial interests which sometimes run contrary to the interests of the government. The Russian government wants to maintain control over Turkmen outlets for political reasons and is therefore seeking an early agreement to have Turkmen gas transported across Russian territory to Ukraine. Gazprom, on the other hand, pursues its commercial interests. These include demanding a higher price for Turkmen gas in transit to Ukraine, and excluding Turkmenistan from becoming a competitor on the Turkish market. Gazprom's attitude is, however, stimulating Central Asia to make yet more determined efforts to search for alternative outlets.

Two examples further illustrate this conflict of interests. In 1994 Lukoil had already been granted a 10 per cent stake in the Chirag and Azeri fields and was negotiating the right to develop Guneshli and Kyapaz. At that time the Russian Foreign Ministry had declared that until the legal status of the Caspian Sea was regulated, Russian companies should not participate in any projects. It claimed that earlier treaties between the Soviet Union and Iran were still valid and that therefore no state could exploit resources unilaterally. A clear contradiction arose between Lukoil and the Russian Fuel and Energy Ministry on the one hand, and the Russian Foreign Ministry on the other. In the end Prime Minister Chernomyrdin and President Yeltsin supported Lukoil's view.

The second example is from July 1997 when the above-mentioned accord was signed by Lukoil and Rosneft together with the Azeri company SOCAR to explore and develop Kyapaz in a disputed area in the Caspian Sea. Within a month Rosneft and Lukoil were forced to withdraw as a conflict had developed in their relations with Turkmenistan, and President Yeltsin and the Russian Foreign Ministry had to apologize to Turkmenistan. In the second case it is obvious that while the Russian companies had embarked on what they considered a commercially viable course, the Ministry of Foreign Affairs had to take political and diplomatic aspects into consideration. In this instance the ministry's position prevailed.

The Russian government's first reaction to the evolving international interest in

Caspian and Central Asian oil and gas resources was to obstruct the implementation of projects. As commercial interest among Russian companies grows, it is colliding with the interest of the Russian government, which is thus coming under pressure to change its position and policy. The change of Russia's position on the division of the Caspian seabed into national sectors is an example of successful lobbying by the oil companies.

8 PROSPECTS FOR THE FUTURE

The rules of the game over influence and control in Central Asia have changed. Today it is no longer political or military but economic means that count as the independent Central Asian states seek partners and investors to develop their countries. To what extent has Russia been able to adapt to this situation and change its policy in order to gain influence and establish control?

The Russian foreign policy consensus of 1993 had included a determination to integrate the former Soviet territories, to become a regional leader and to deny out-of-region states influence there. In 1993 Russia looked upon its relations with the Central Asian states mainly from a zero-sum perspective, as a necessary buffer zone and the backyard of its own great-power status. The policy of the Russian government was mostly contradictory with regard to efforts to integrate Central Asia: its economic policy distanced Central Asia, while using political and military means in an attempt to anchor Central Asia within the CIS.

The second term of Yeltsin's presidency and the new Russian government of 'young reformers' gave new impetus to economic reforms. Russia became less willing to pay the military and political costs required by a geopolitically oriented strategy. The government instead became more prone to seek pragmatic solutions to practical problems. Such a policy change had already started to take place during 1996 as a way to bridge the gap that had developed in 1993–5 between high-flown declarations of economic and military integration under Russian leadership, and reality. As a consequence of its own weakness and lack of capabilities, Russia was forced into a more low-profile policy towards the CIS territories.

Russia continued its efforts to develop multilateral as well as bilateral integration with Central Asia, but was not successful. In 1997 it became evident that multilateral integration had reached a dead end. The interests of the Central Asian states had diverged from those of Russia to such an extent that even the most loyal of them, Kazakhstan, openly criticized Russian policy and CIS integration. The state of multilateral relations was similarly reflected in bilateral relations. During 1997 disputes between Russia and Kazakhstan came into the open. Since 1996 Uzbekistan and Turkmenistan had cast themselves as the front-runners in Central Asia in seeking to reduce dependence on Russia and to increase contacts with other states. Even small Kyrgyzstan and war-torn Tajikistan, both dependent on Russia for security, started to reorient their contacts, especially within the commercial field.

Russian policy was paralysed in the sense that the government was incapable of revising its policy sufficiently to attract the Central Asians. Economic strength and economic means now counted more than military and political predominance, and Russia had less to offer in this respect. The riches of the oil and gas resources of the independent Central Asian states attracted foreign governments and investors. They thereby encouraged the Central Asians in their efforts to become partners in larger and wider international networks. Russia had to see its own influence in Central Asia being eroded and its position undermined as the Central Asians diversified their contacts with the outside world.

In 1997 a geo-economic orientation had become more evident in Russian policy. It was reflected in statements in November 1997 by the then Deputy Prime Minister Nemtsov calling for more active Russian involvement in the development of the Caspian oilfields to counter growing Western influence in the region. Russia's new focus on energy issues reflects its awareness that the rules of the game had changed as regards acquiring influence and control in Central Asia. Russian companies are partners in most of the main international projects for the exploitation of oil and gas in the Caspian and Central Asia. However, Russia is not economically strong enough to compete successfully with Western and Asian companies as an investor and financier. The new Russian focus on energy issues can therefore be viewed as an effort to concentrate resources and efforts on a few key sectors vital for maintaining Russian control over Central Asia.

However, to what extent can the Russian government be given credit for this change in policy? Russian policy-making since the break-up of the Soviet Union has been described as fragmented in the sense that there is no central authority. Powerful interest and lobby groups have become more influential in the policy-making process. The military's influence was, from the early 1990s, gradually replaced by economic lobby groups, the most important of which were the huge gas and oil companies. By the end of 1997 Gazprom had become so powerful and active that the Russian media commented that it had usurped the government's foreign policy initiative and had taken over the role of the Foreign Ministry.

Common interests characterize Gazprom's relations with the Russian government. It was not only Prime Minister Viktor Chernomyrdin, a former director of Gazprom with large interests in the company, who guaranteed such access to the government. '"Gas diplomacy" has been and remains one of the most important elements of Russian policy towards the CIS, and Gazprom plays a central role in this,' wrote one analyst.[1]

---

[1] Yakov Pappe, 'Neftyanaya gazovaya diplomatiya Rossii', *Pro et Contra* (Moscow), no. 3, summer 1997, p. 57.

Gazprom's director Rem Vyakhirev accompanies the president and the prime minister on many of their most important foreign visits. The company has a unique position not only because it is responsible for 95 per cent of all Russian gas exploitation and all gas transport but also because it is the largest gas company in the world.

The state and the gas and oil industry share the same objective with regard to the former Soviet territories: to create an integrated economic region over which Russia has control. However, the Russian companies within the energy sector also have specific interests of their own. In general one can hardly talk about overlapping foreign policy interests between the Russian government and companies. The oil companies act independently from the Russian government and the Foreign Ministry, sometimes with embarrassing consequences for the latter.

The Russian government and the commercial companies have been talking with different voices on sensitive foreign policy issues, thereby contributing to the confusion over what constitutes Russian foreign policy. The companies have aimed at what they have considered to be economically sound goals. A similar process is taking place with regard to local leaders in the Russian regions. The regions act independently to promote their own narrow interests and to secure stability and economic growth by developing contacts and exchanges with neighbouring or more distant regions. They share an economic and result-oriented approach and do not give much consideration to any national strategic perspective.

A 'cooperative perspective' with an economic strategy is reflected in the public debate, but still mainly at a theoretical and academic level. Recommendations in the press for better legal conditions and support for Russian business fall into this category. In Russian academic analyses of the situation in Central Asia it is pointed out that Russian business has to behave independently from the state in order not to be identified with Russian state politics or 'integrationist' politicians. One researcher claims that as long as Russian business is not able to separate itself from the business of the state, the Central Asians will continue to look upon it with suspicion and avoid dealing with its representatives.[2]

The processes that are evolving in Central Asia today will result in a very different political landscape a few years from now. Russia has lost its dominant position and has no chance of regaining it.

The financial and political crisis in Russia that erupted following the *de facto* devaluation of the rouble on 17 August 1998, the default on internal debt and the moratorium on foreign debt will speed up Russia's 'involuntary disengagement' from Central Asia. With domestic production falling and the rouble undermined,

[2] O. Reznikova, 'Rossiya, Turtsiya i Iran v Tsentralnoi Azii', *Mirovaya ekonomika i mezhdunarodnye otnosheniya*, 1997, no. 1.

Russia will be preoccupied with bring its own houses in order. The new prime minister, Yevgeny Primakov, managed to prevent the situation from running out of control, but his choice of government indicated an economic policy hampered by political compromises.

As the crisis developed the Central Asian leaders tried to play down the effects on their national economies. Yet they will probably increase their efforts to expand their other external economic relations to avoid being drawn into the Russian crisis. By the time Russia regains any strength, the Central Asian states will already have secured a considerably more diverse set of external relations with Asian and Western countries.

The factors behind these processes are beyond Russian control and Russia does not have the capacity to reverse them. The only way for it to secure a future role in Central Asian politics is to accept the continuing reorientation of the region, to develop normal economic relations, and to become attractive to Central Asia on the basis of mutual interests. From what has been said above, Russian private companies and Russian regions may play a role in paving the way for such a policy.